BRADFORD W.G. PUBLIC LIBRARY

3 3328 00049580 0

P9-CQQ-344

Donated to the Library
through a generous gift
to

Book Funds

from

Bette Northover

BRADFORD WG LIBRARY
100 HOLLAND COURT, BOX 130
BRADFORD, ONT. L3Z 2A7

Water Gardening
with
Derek Fell

Water Gardening

with

Derek Fell

Practical Advice and
Personal Favorites
from the Best-Selling Author
and Television Show Host

DISCARDED
BRADFORD WG
PUBLIC LIBRARY

FRIEDMAN/FAIRFAX
P U B L I S H E R S

BRADFORD WG LIBRARY
100 HOLLAND COURT, BOX 130
BRADFORD, ONT. L3Z 2A7

A FRIEDMAN/FAIRFAX BOOK

© 1998 by Michael Friedman Publishing Group, Inc.

All rights reserved. No part of this publication may be reproduced, stored in a retrieval system, or transmitted, in any form or by any means, electronic, mechanical, photocopying, recording, or otherwise, without prior written permission from the publisher.

Library of Congress Cataloging-in-Publication Data

Fell, Derek.
    Water gardening with Derek Fell / by Derek Fell.
       p.   cm.
    Includes bibliographical references (p.   ) and index.
    ISBN 1-56799-556-X
    1. Water gardens. 2. Aquatic plants.   I. Title
SB423.F45 1998
635.9'674—dc21   97-34777
                                                     CIP

Editors: Susan Lauzau, Penelope O'Sullivan
Art Director: Jeff Batzli
Layout Designer: Meredith Miller
Photography Editor: Christopher C. Bain
Production Manager: Camille Lee

Color separations by Colourscan Overseas Co Pte Ltd.
Printed in Singapore by Tien Wah Press (PTE) Limited

1 3 5 7 9 10 8 6 4 2

For bulk purchases and special sales, please contact:
Friedman/Fairfax Publishers
Attention: Sales Department
15 West 26th Street
New York, New York 10010
212/685-6610 FAX 212/685-1307

Visit our website:
http://www.metrobooks.com

Frontispiece: A small pool surrounded by serene plantings creates a tranquil garden spot.

Dedication

For my three children, Christina, Victoria, and Derek Jr.,
all of whom love gardening.

Acknowledgments

In recent years I have enjoyed creating a series of twenty-five theme gardens at my home, Cedaridge Farm, in Bucks County, Pennsylvania. Many of them feature water in the form of ponds, pools, streams, waterfalls, and boggy areas. Words of advice and inspiration during the construction of these areas have come from many sources, especially from Springbrook Nurseries in Shamong, New Jersey, where most of the step-by-step photography for this book was taken.

Much inspiration was also taken from visiting Claude Monet's wonderful water garden in Giverny, France. However, the individual who has taught me more about the magic of water than anyone is garden designer Hiroshi Makita. Trained in a Zen Buddhist monastery in Japan, Hiroshi specializes in designing and installing traditional Japanese water gardens in the Philadelphia area. Many of his designs are featured in this book.

The success of my own garden, however, would not be possible without the help of my wife, Carolyn, and my grounds supervisor, Wendy Fields, who ensures that the water gardens are always picture-perfect. Also, my sincere thanks to Kathy Nelson, my office manager, who helps to keep my extensive photo library organized. Through her attention to detail we maintain accurate pictorial records of everything that grows at Cedaridge Farm.

Contents

Opposite: A serene Japanese-style garden is planted along a slow-moving stream.

Left: A narrow, arching stream of water called a "silver thread" cascades into a small sheltered pool. Above: An English-style rock garden featuring a series of informal pools commands attention on a sunny slope at Cedaridge farm.

Introduction

All life on earth begins in water. Plants, animals, and humans cannot live without it. Both the sight and the sound of sparkling water uplift our senses. Water has many unique qualities besides refreshment. It is the only element on earth that can change from solid to liquid to vaporous form as a consequence of slight changes in temperature. Above 32°F (0°C), water turns from ice to cool liquid. As the temperature rises, the liquid evaporates as mist or steam, causing rainbows when the sun shines. Water also has a profound physical influence on the substances it touches, making stonework shine, turning morning dew frosty, and helping plants to maintain a lush, healthy, green appearance. Water can be a powerful force, turning mill wheels to produce energy and causing horrendous erosion if uncontrolled. When water is scarce, the effect can be devastating, turning soil dust-dry, killing plants, and creating deserts.

Water is the music of nature, like birdsong. No one knows how to play water's musical keyboard better than the Japanese. They cascade water from a great height to produce a thunderous noise accompanied by clouds of spray and mist. They tumble it in a series of naturalistic waterfalls and rock pools, regulating the flow and fall to produce a symphony of sounds as the water gushes, splashes, gurgles, or slaps against rocks.

They ripple it over shallows where it gleams and glitters in the sunlight. To the Japanese Zen garden masters, the control of water is an art and a science, most evident when they use water as a mirror to reflect the silvery moon in the dark of night.

Still water can double the visual pleasure of its surroundings, reflecting pool plantings, arched bridges, and snow-capped mountains. On cloudy days when the surface turns opaque, water can produce a mysterious, sinister quality. Even in the confined space of a small garden, the presence of water can be introduced in a variety of ingenious ways: as a gurgling fountain,

Moss-covered rocks beside a spillway, together with feathery ferns growing along a natural stream, evoke a tranquil feeling. Constant moisture is necessary to produce luxurious moss and fern growth like this.

a glittering rill, a sinuous millrace, or a rushing stream. Perhaps the best way to introduce water to a garden is by means of a waterfall that tumbles into a reflecting pool filled with goldfish.

It is not necessary to have an existing source of water for pools, streams, or waterfalls. Many of the finest water gardens are fed by a recirculating pump that provides a constant flow of water through them, regardless of natural rainfall or natural springs. Even residents of a desert, therefore, can have an oasis of water and greenery.

These rocks, carefully situated along a narrow stream, direct water to the left or right, creating a series of naturalistic cascades. Musical sounds from their splashing fills the garden.

Lucky is the property owner with an existing waterfall on-site. Since that likelihood is rare, perhaps nothing in all of landscape design is more satisfying—or more challenging—than designing and constructing a waterfall. Zen gardeners value the presence of waterfalls so highly that there is a whole vocabulary of symbolic terms to describe desirable features. For example, a heavy flow that creates a curtain of water is called "silver fleece" or "falling cloth," and a light flow broken by boulders to make strands of falling water is "silver threads." Zen gardeners also study local natural water courses for ideas to heighten the allure of a rocky stream or waterfall. Rocks covered in moss are collected from the wild and placed strategically along streams and rock ledges splashed with spray. Pieces of driftwood or weather-worn dead trees are placed along the margin of a stream for decorative effect and to hold pockets of soil for colonies of water iris, bog primulas, and marsh marigolds. By interrupting the descent of water along a stream with boulders and by adjusting the height of rock ledges, water can be guided to the left or right, cascading in a series of steps to create a musical rhythm.

At my home, Cedaridge Farm, we have several wonderful water gardens, including a marsh garden with bog-loving plants, a water lily pond rimmed with perennial plants, and a small rock garden featuring pools formed by rigid liners that cascade water from one pool to another. Occupying a space barely 10 by 10 feet (3 by 3m), this water feature was a do-it-yourself project and took only a weekend to install.

When we decided to grow water lilies for our pond we chose hardy kinds, as they tend to take care of themselves provided their roots remain below the ice line. Tropicals, however, need to be moved indoors to overwinter in a heated holding tank. We also maintain waterlilies in tubs on a deck. We pay special attention to creating pleasing color harmonies, notably blue and yellow, which we foster by growing lots of irises. Red, pink, and silver is another combination we find effective. Though most silver-leaf plants are from dry areas and demand good drainage, we have found both lamb's ears (*Stachys byzantina*) and variegated maiden grass (*Miscanthus sinensis* 'Variegatus') to be tolerant of moist soil. These plants make good silvery backgrounds against which to view red and pink hibiscus, astilbes, and cardinal flowers.

One of the most beautiful water gardens I ever saw was a small waterlily pond surrounded by large boulders. Overhead, a bamboo pipe arched a jet of water onto rocks at the edge of the pool. The water splayed out into large droplets as it reached the stones, then splintered into a spray so fine it produced clouds of mist and a brilliant double rainbow. Ah, to have a water garden designed for a rainbow! Be warned—water gardens are addictive.

Planning a
Water Garden

Opposite: This small, informal water garden features a nymph that pours recirculated water into the pool.

All water garden designs can be classified as formal or informal, with informal garden designs by far the most popular. The first question to ask is: How big? Rather like choosing a greenhouse or conservatory addition, the answer is

An Italian-style water garden at Blake House, owned by the University of California at Berkeley, features a formal waterlily pool that leads the eye back to a grotto.

usually "as big as possible" (within the constraints of cost and space). Of course, in deciding the size of your water feature, consideration should also be given to a sense of scale, making sure that the size of the water feature is in proportion to its surroundings. Remember that there are miniature varieties of waterlilies for small pools, since a regular-size waterlily can occupy 25 square feet (2.3 sq m) of space with its large, floating, rounded leaves.

Formal water gardens are usually square, round, oval, or rectangular in shape. They can be part of outdoor garden rooms or can extend the architecture of a building. These geometric pools are often found in city courtyards or adjacent to period homes built in the French renaissance or Italian baroque styles. The lines of these pools echo the style of the nearby building and walls. However, highly formal pool designs can look sensational as surprise elements—especially as sunken gardens—in woodland settings.

Informal water gardens have a natural look. To design one you should study natural ponds, streams, and waterfalls in your area. It is easy to make mistakes and end up with a contrived appearance when combining rocks, plants, and water. With waterfalls, for example, you will notice that few in nature are composed of small stones, which easily wash away. For stability and longevity, waterfalls generally feature some large dominant boulders that only a front-end loader can lift into position. A big mistake (unless the pool is small and uses rigid liners) is to design water features that restrict the size of rocks to what one person can carry.

In the wild, notice the tilt of boulders bordering streams and ponds. Some produce natural overhangs like observation platforms, and colonies of plants grow among pockets of soil or silt between the rocks. Notice how some plants (such as ivy, ferns, and creeping Jenny) have a fleece-like quality, not only covering flat boulders but extending over the edge and dipping their stems into the water. Observe the way that many streams are naturally crossed by fallen logs and edged with weathered tree roots resembling driftwood. Make sketches of the features that most impress you as you investigate natural ponds and streams, and try to emulate them in your water garden.

Above: Set in a serene Japanese-style garden, this kidney-shaped informal pool is in keeping with the controlled naturalness of the space. Below: A beautiful cloud-shaped waterlily pool graces the Ladew Topiary Gardens in Maryland. Symmetrical or geometric shapes are characteristic of formal pools.

Professional Help

Construction workers who take pride in their work live by a creed: "It takes less effort to prevent a problem than it does to solve a problem." That is perhaps more true of water garden features than anything else, since the smallest mistake, such as a crack in the liner or a muskrat hole near a spillway, can quickly drain a pond and require an expensive, monumental effort to fix. If you plan to use a rigid pond liner, you can probably do the job yourself. But if you have a large job that requires a flexible liner, you should hire an experienced contractor to do it, preferably one with pond-building experience, since you do not want the frustration of a contractor learning by trial and error on your project. Believe me, many people have suffered through that nightmare!

How Much Does a Pond Cost?

This depends on the size and volume of your pond and its complexity. A professional installation including grading and a backhoe to dig the hole, a large flexible liner as a seal, stonework around the edging to anchor the liner, and a basic selection of plants could cost the same as installing a similarly sized swimming pool. About 90 percent of the cost of pond installations is for labor. Small pools using rigid or flexible liners cost a lot less, since you can install them yourself, saving the major expense of paid labor. On top of the liner and installation fee is the cost of plants. Think of water gardening as a stimulating hobby, like building a train set or collecting stamps. A beautiful pond or pool is something you will never tire of admiring. It may also add value to your property.

Site Analysis

If the lie of the land is firm, flat, and sunny, with shelter from windbreaks and a clay soil that can be dug easily, you have a perfect situation for a water feature. Unfortunately, most people do not have that perfect set of circumstances, and if they do it's usually not where they want to put a water feature. Rather, they want to put it in shade or on the lowest part of the property in a boggy area. The majority of ponds, pools, and streams end up being installed in either shade or swampy soil—both considered problem sites.

Above: A natural rocky slope has been used to create a series of cascades; the water is recirculated continuously.
Below: Occasional pruning of overhead branches keeps this site lightly shaded so that flowering plants, such as irises and azaleas, will bloom.

Shade

Shade presents a problem because there are tree roots to work around. If you do not want to lose the existing trees, you may need to move them aside and "park" them until you can put them back into places that do not interfere with the pond or the pond liner. Shade also presents a maintenance problem because leaves fall in, clog filters, and produce a putrid mess at the bottom. Shade also inhibits good flowering, although there are some shade-loving water plants.

Low-Lying Areas

Low-lying areas, such as places that puddle water after it rains or that are permanently boggy, can present problems from back-pressure—the natural tendency for water under a heavy weight to push up, causing soil movement and jeopardizing the stability of the liner. Usually, low-lying areas will need good drainage through pipes sunk into ditches at strategic points to drain away excess moisture. These ditches may also need to be lined with filter fabric to trap silt and comply with local ordinances.

Low-lying sites frequently suffer from heavy runoff during rain, thunderstorms, and snow melt, converging in a relentless downhill flow that can quickly damage pond and stream banks. A series of terraces or catchments may be necessary to drain floodwater away from any low-lying water features.

Regardless of its position, a site markup should be done before any ground breaking occurs. "Site markup" is a term used in local ordinances requiring identification of underground septic lines and power lines.

In analyzing your site you should also examine whether the water feature will pose an "attractive nuisance" to children, a legal term that makes you responsible for any

Above: Snakeweed (*Polygonum bistorta* 'Superbum'), here planted to form a colony around the margin of a natural pond, flowers in early summer. Below: Another early summer–flowering plant for pondsides is false spiraea (*Astilbe* × *arendsii*). Both thrive in humus-rich boggy soil.

harm to children, even if they trespass. Local ordinances will often specify a depth of no more than 3 feet (90cm), or sometimes less, for a pond as a child safety feature. Other ordinances may stipulate that a water feature must be fenced off. Since pools and ponds are a magnet for children, you may want to consider placing these features in a position that is well hidden from view.

Pond Materials and Accessories

Though you would not think it from the hundreds of pages of equipment featured in water garden catalogs, "keep it simple" is sound advice for most water features. Indeed, the ideal situation is to dispense with anything, including filters and pumps, that can clog, rust, leak, short out, or break down. A crystal-clear pond is possible by using natural water filters like oxygenating plants and fish. There are, however, certain essentials that are indispensable. First and foremost is the actual pond liner. Though there are many ponds and water courses that do not use liners (mostly clay-lined ponds that have been pounded with a machine to create a seal), these are subject to damage, especially from muskrats, turtles, and snakes making submerged holes. The two most commonly used methods to seal a water feature today are preformed rigid liners for small pools and flexible liners for large ones.

Pool Edgings

Be creative with pool edgings, especially raised ones, since edging styles can match your garden's theme. For example, a Florida or California courtyard pool might look good with an edging of Spanish tile.

For natural edgings, look beyond the obvious choice of boulders and stones. Consider taking grass down to the edge, breaking up portions with hummocks of closely clipped boxwood and azaleas to resemble wind-shorn shrubs. Gnarled old tree trunks laid on their sides with hollows for sprouting colonies of creeping phlox and ferns are appropriate. Wooden pegs are popular edgings for Japanese gardens.

Small pools are easilly installed with rigid pond liners or by sinking a large container into the ground. Either method offers a welcome opportunity to grow lush water plants.

Rigid Pond Liners

For small pools, there are many styles of preformed rigid liners that are relatively easy to install. Rigid liners are more expensive than flexible ones, though neither is exorbitantly priced. The extra cost of a rigid liner is generally worth the convenience even though the available shapes are fairly standard (see diagrams on page 47). Rigid liners are generally made from fiberglass or rigid plastic (polyethylene). Fiberglass is the strongest, longest-lasting, and most expensive liner material. The most important point when installing a rigid liner is to give it a snug fit. Avoid digging deeper than you must and then backfilling, because there is always shrinkage and settling when backfilling. Also, keep the liner lip perfectly level, since any tilting will be evident along the waterline when the liner is filled with water.

As a base for rigid liners, consider using wet newspapers or old carpeting between the liner and indigenous soil. Also use a ¼-inch (6mm) thickness of wet newspapers around the sides of rigid liners for protection from side pressure.

Step-by-Step Installation of a Rigid Liner

The following sequence, which was photographed at Cedaridge Farm, shows a small water garden from beginning of installation to the finished product. This small-space water garden took only a weekend to install and plant.

1. Using a flexible garden hose, outline the shape of your rigid liner.

2. Dig a hole to match the contours of the liner.

3. Place the rigid liner in its hole and check for a level top with a spirit level.

4. Backfill the edges of the liner with sand to cushion the sides.

5. Anchor the edges of the liner with gravel to ensure stability, then fill liner with water.

6. Rim the edges with flat stones, making sure they overlap the liner so that it is shaded and hidden from view.

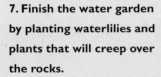

7. Finish the water garden by planting waterlilies and plants that will creep over the rocks.

Flexible Pond Liners

There are two choices of aquaculture membranes today—45-mil EPDM (a type of rubber) and 30-mil PVC (polyvinyl chloride). Unfortunately, PVC earned a bad reputation for leakages during its infancy because too thin a grade was being used. Today, however, it is considered the best of the two alternatives. First, it is lighter in weight than the EPDM equivalent and therefore easier to lay in place. And the tensile strength is better than EPDM, as it will stretch 300 percent compared to EPDM's 200 percent. It has 200 pounds per inch (90kg per 2.5cm) of tear resistance compared to EPDM's 150 pounds per inch (68kg per 2.5cm).

Though PVC has less tolerance to low temperatures than EPDM, it is still highly tolerant, failing to break down at -22°F (-30°C) compared to -56°F (-49°C). Unlike EPDM, PVC is not a crystalline product, making it highly resistant to ozone degradation. However, it is susceptible to ultraviolet degradation and must be completely covered against exposure to UV rays. This is standard procedure with pond liners anyway, because it is most desirable to hide them from view.

PVC is easily seamed so that, for unusually large areas, two or more rolls can be locked together to make a strong weld, while EPDM adhesive seams are unreliable. Also, PVC is recyclable, while EPDM is not.

To calculate the amount of liner needed, not only do the contours of the pond need to be taken into account, but the liner must extend for a good distance beyond the edges to be weighted down with edging rocks for a tight seal.

Since the weight of the water keeps the pond liner firmly in place, there is no need for any other form of anchorage like stones or gravel. However, loose stones on the bottom do have a tendency to protect the pond from deer should they step into the pond for a drink or a nibble of waterlily foliage. Since frost heaving and subsurface water pressure can push up stones, which can puncture a liner, lay a 2-inch (5cm) layer of sand underneath the liner.

After a flexible liner is anchored with flagstones, poolside plants such as hostas and sweet flag can be placed in pockets of soil to soften the hard lines of the stone.

Step-by-Step Installation of a Flexible Liner

Use a flexible liner when you need a pool that is beyond the maximum size of a rigid liner (usually 6 feet [1.5m] in length).

1. Mark out the shape of your pool with a flexible hose.

2. Dig the hole, creating ledges for submerged pots containing marginal plants.

3. Check for level surface with a spirit level and measure the contours for the correct size of liner, allowing for an extra 2 feet (60cm) of liner all around.

4. Spread the liner in the hole and weight down the sides with blocks.

5. Rim the edge with flat stones.

6. Place a recirculating pump in the deepest part of the pool. Hide hose inlet with movable stones.

7. Fill pool with water in two stages—one-third full to settle the liner before adding the stone rim, then fill to the top when ready to place plants.

8. Place plants appropriately— waterlilies for the center, marginal plants for the edge, bog plants around the sides.

9. Add fish to the finished pool. As plants mature they will fill in initial gaps.

Do I Need a Pump?

You'll require a pump only if you need to recirculate water to create a stream, cascade, or fountain. Recirculating water for a stream effect will take a bigger pump than you would need for a fountain. The choice of pump also depends on whether you have mechanical filtration, no filtration, or a biological filtration system. The size of the pond is also vital. Consult a water pump supplier for the right choice. Choose a good brand name noted for high performance and low operating cost, like Oase or Little Giant. Be aware that submersible pumps require an electrical source, and the intake will need checking at intervals to keep it clear of debris. The pump's impeller may need cleaning every two months.

A raised formal pool creates a transitional design element between a raised patio and a sunken lawn area. Potted plants help to decorate the edges of the pool. A pump powers the high-arching fountain.

Do I Need a Filter?

You won't need a filter if you have the right balance of oxygenating plants and aquatic life. A pond or pool can be a completely self-contained environment with self-cleaning systems. To achieve a natural balance, a good formula for every 11 square feet (1 sq m) of surface is two clumps of oxygenating plants (preferably each clump planted in a sunken pot) plus one large waterlily, a dozen snails, and two fish.

If your pond will not stay clear regardless of the number of submerged plants you have, then you will need to consider a filter. Filtering cleans up debris, algae, and fish wastes that cloud the water. Mechanical filters trap the unwanted material onto filter pads for easy removal. Your aquatic specialist will help you choose the proper filter for your water feature. There are three choices: a small bubble filter ideal for pools of up to three hundred gallons (1,135L), a pond filter that can be used with a pump in or out of the pond, and a biological filter. Biological filters are tub-like units positioned outside the pond. They must be placed higher than the water level of the pond since water is gravity-fed through levels of gravel where nitrifying bacteria consume the waste matter. The filter is maintained by flushing water down through the gravel one to four times monthly, depending on the number of fish in your pond.

Above: This city garden design contrasts a formal pool edge with informal surroundings. Below: This entirely informal pond in a rural setting was created by using a flexible liner. Though these pools are quite different in character, neither requires a filter because plants, fish, and snails combine to keep the water clear.

Growing
Water Garden Plants

Opposite: A stepped waterfall introduces water into a small, plant-filled pool.

This naturalistic waterlily pond is fed by a rill that helps to recirculate water from the pond to a rise of ground a hundred yards upstream.

Types of
Water Plants

There are six kinds of water plants you should consider for water gardens. Except for the floating plants, all can grow in the mud at the bottom or along the margins of pools. Since most aquatic plants have vigorous spreading root systems, it is always best if they are confined to pots. Set the pots at the proper level by placing them on plant stands, such as metal milk crates, heavy inverted clay pots, or house bricks. The ideal water garden includes a balance of each plant type, not only because this ensures a healthy microenvironment for clear water but also because it is aesthetically pleasing to see a variety of foliage forms.

Floating Plants

Floating plants such as parrot's feather and water lettuce are water purifiers that take their nutrients directly from the water. They float on the surface, adding color, texture, and variety, while providing shade and shelter for fish. They don't do well in flowing streams, except in quiet eddies, because any strong water current can sweep them away. In pools and ponds some floating plants can become highly invasive. In some states the more aggressive floating plants like water lettuce and water hyacinth are banned,

Above left: Water lettuce is a popular floating plant. Above: A small entrance planting features a rich assortment of water plants around a free-form pool.

since in a frost-free environment they can produce 600,000 offspring within six months. However, they are easy to control in a small water garden, especially one that experiences frost. Some floating plants, like parrot's feather, need their roots anchored in soil, but others, like water hyacinth, do not. Floating plants are usually bought bare-root and should be set in place in spring, after danger of frost.

Duckweed is a hardy floating plant that often finds its way into ponds as a stowaway on roots and in the pots of other aquatic plants you buy. Goldfish eat it as food, and it helps control the growth of algae. Do not allow it to completely cover the water and block out light. Excess growth of any floating plant should be scooped up in a net and delegated to the compost pile. In the following list, tender floating plants are marked with an asterisk. Those that need to be rooted in soil have a ❧ sign.

Eichhornia crassipes (water hyacinth)*
Lemna minor (duckweed)
Ludwigia peploides (mosaic plant)*
Lysimachia nummularia (creeping Jenny)❧
Myriophyllum aquaticum (parrot's feather)❧
Pistia stratiotes (water lettuce)*

Shallow Marginal Plants

These plants, such as arrowhead, grow in up to 12 inches (30cm) of water. They mostly have upright or fountainlike foliage that softens the edges of a pond and contrasts well with the horizontal rounded foliage of waterlilies. Both shallow marginal plants and deep marginal plants provide an essential nesting habitat for waterfowl such as ducks and swans, and both can be purchased as bareroot transplants and potted. In the following list, all plants will also grow in boggy soil. They do not need their roots permanently covered with water. Tender varieties are marked with an asterisk.

Acorus calamus (sweet flag)

Caltha palustris (marsh marigold)

Canna hybrids (canna)*

Carex elata 'Bowles Golden' (Bowles golden grass)

Colocasia esculenta (elephant's ear)*

Cyperus alternifolius (umbrella palm)*

Equisetum hyemale (horsetail)

Houttuynia cordata (chameleon plant)

Hydrocleys nymphoides (water poppy)*

Iris ensata (Japanese iris)

Iris, Louisiana hybrids (Louisiana iris)

Iris versicolor (blue flag iris)

Juncus effusus (corkscrew rush)

Ludwigia peploides (mosaic plant)

Nymphoides indica (water snowflake)*

Sagittaria latifolia (arrowhead)

Above: Bog-loving plants—such as sweet flag (center)—like their roots submerged in shallow water. Below: Flag irises will tolerate deep water over their roots.

Deep Marginal Plants

These plants—such as cattails, pickerel weed, and flag irises—have upright foliage that's usually spiky or spear shaped. These generally grow tall and can be planted up to 2 feet (60cm) deep. In the following list, tender varieties are marked with an asterisk.

Cyperus papyrus (Egyptian papyrus)*

Iris pseudacorus (yellow flag iris)

Pontederia cordata (pickerel weed)

Taxodium distichum (bald cypress)

Thalia dealbata (water canna)

Typha latifolia (cattail)

Bog Plants

Bog plants can survive long periods with their roots covered with water but prefer a moist or boggy soil. These include Japanese primroses, pitcher plants, and cardinal flowers. They like pond edges, with their roots slightly above the permanent waterline. In the water garden, they make the transition between plants that grow in water and those that need higher ground for good drainage. Bog plants are usually purchased potted, though some are sold as bareroot transplants. In the following list, tender plants are marked with an asterisk.

Alchemilla mollis (lady's mantle)

Arum italicum (Italian arum)

Aruncus dioicus (goatsbeard)

Astilbe × *arendsii* (false spiraea)

Betula nigra 'Heritage' (heritage birch)

Darlingtonia californica (cobra lily)*

Eupatorium purpureum (Joe-Pye weed)

Gunnera manicata (Chilean rhubarb)

Heracleum mantegazzianum (giant hogweed)

Hibiscus moscheutos (swamp hibiscus)

Hosta sieboldiana 'Elegans' (blue hosta)

Ilex verticillata (winterberry)

Ligularia dentata 'Othello' (ragwort)

Lobelia cardinalis (cardinal flower)

Lysichiton americanum (yellow skunk cabbage)

Matteuccia struthiopteris (ostrich fern)

Metasequoia glyptostroboides (dawn redwood)

Miscanthus sinensis 'Variegatus' (variegated Japanese silver grass)

Myosotis scorpioides (water forget-me-not)

Peltiphyllum peltatum (umbrella plant)

Petasites japonicus 'Gigantea' (giant Japanese coltsfoot)

Primula japonica (Japanese primrose)

Primula × *beesiana* (candelabra primrose)

Sarracenia leucophylla (pitcher plant)*

The edges of this stream are richly planted with primroses and hostas. In the soil higher up the bank, where drainage is better, foxgloves have naturalized.

Waterlilies and Lotuses

Waterlilies and lotuses have large leaves that can be the highlight for a water garden, as Claude Monet demonstrated with his water garden at Giverny. Waterlilies are classified as hardies (these survive northern winters) or tropicals (these need to overwinter in heated holding tanks in areas with severe frosts). Although hardies tolerate freezing temperatures, their roots must remain below the expected ice line. If there is any danger of ice reaching the roots, pots should be lowered to the bottom of the pond and raised in spring. Ironically, in northern gardens the blooming of hardy waterlilies dwindles in early September. They do not have as long a blooming season as tropicals, which can continue for another two months. Also, tropicals are larger-flowered and offer a wider color range, including blue, which is completely absent among hardy waterlilies. Some tropicals are classified as evening bloomers because they start to open in the late afternoon and close by 10 A.M. the following morning.

Hardy waterlilies are not as large-flowered as tropicals and their flowers float on the water, while tropicals have flowers measuring up to 10 inches (25cm) across, and always hold their flowers erect up to 9 inches (22.5cm) above the water surface on slender stems. Among both types there are miniatures suitable for growing in small pools and in tubs. Both waterlilies and lotuses have aggressive tuberous roots. Purchased from a local aquatic center, these plants are mostly sold in pots. When purchased by mail, however, you generally receive a bareroot division wrapped in moist shredded newspaper and waxed paper to keep it from drying out. Because the number of waterlily and lotus varieties is extensive, the following list is of shade-tolerant varieties only. Tropicals are indicated with an asterisk.

'Albert Greenberg'*
'Attraction'
'Comanche'
'Chromatella'
'Director Moore'*
'Helvola'*
'St. Louis Gold'*

This large formal pool features tropical waterlilies (foreground) and lotuses. Tropical waterlilies, unlike hardy species, hold their heads above the water.

Submerged Plants

Also called oxygenators, submerged plants live their whole lives underwater, though some varieties—like dwarf arrowhead—send their flowers up to the surface. They compete with algae for the same nutrients, keeping pond water clear and controlling the spread of algae. Their feathery or straplike leaves create sheltered spawning areas for fish. Since they are delicate plants, easily disturbed when planted in pond mud, they are best introduced into the pond in submerged pots covered with a fine wire mesh cone to prevent fish, waterfowl, and mammals from disturbing them. In the following list, all are considered hardy.

Cabomba caroliniana (cabomba)

Elodea canadensis (anacharis)

Myriophyllum aquaticum (parrot's feather)

Vallisneria americana (vallisneria)

Parrot's feather is an example of a submerged plant that extends its tips above the water, helping to keep a pool or pond clear of algae.

Water plants and plants that like moist soil, such as these hostas, can be purchased from specialist aquatic garden nurseries as transplants.

Where to Buy

If you visit a local nursery that specializes in water plants, you may find it has a fairly good selection of waterlily varieties in pots and only one variety of every other type of water plant. Even at the best aquatic garden centers the choice of plants can be limited. A much greater selection is possible through specialty mail-order suppliers, although plants shipped by mail are generally bareroot transplants.

Variety Selection

Read catalog and plant label descriptions carefully. If possible, join a waterlily society for up-to-date information about species and cultivars, since a careful choice of cultivars can make the difference between a common water garden and a unique one. Take waterlilies as an example. Many cultivars sold today originate from a breeding program by a Frenchman, the late Joseph Bory Latour-Marliac. The painter Claude Monet grew many Marliac varieties in his sensational water garden at Giverny: 'Caroliniana' (pink), 'Chromatella' (yellow), 'Comanche' (orange), and 'Escarboucle' (red). Both 'Chromatella' and 'Comanche' have been identified as shade-tolerant, blooming in as little as 3 hours a day of direct sunlight.

In recent years, the Missouri Botanical Garden in St. Louis has made tremendous strides in breeding tropical waterlilies. 'Director Moore', 'St. Louis Gold', and 'Albert Greenberg' are three recommended for shady areas. Among new lotus cultivars, it is unlikely you will ever find a more beautiful flower than 'Mrs. Perry D. Slocum', which changes from a lovely shade of pink to yellow.

Since waterlily cultivars don't generally grow true from seed, the best way to acquire these cultivars is through purchasing plants or acquiring divisions from friends.

Soil Preparation

When all water plants are grown in containers, no further soil preparation is necessary for the pond itself. If, however, you want a pool or pond rimmed with bog plants as a transitional area, you should create a slightly acid, humus-rich soil capable of retaining moisture and allowing plant roots freedom to roam in their search for nutrients.

To improve pondside soils that contain either too much sand or too much clay, haul in screened topsoil from a nursery and mix in bales of peat, garden compost, and well-decomposed animal manure or well-decomposed leaf mold to improve the humus content. Be careful if you interfere with the existing soil around the pond, as this can make the sides unstable and encourage erosion. Rather, build a raised bed using

Before planting these false spiraeas the ground was dug over and peat moss mixed in to improve its humus content.

boulders or strong tree branches along the pond rim. Raise the soil surface at least 8 to 12 inches (20 to 30cm) above the indigenous soil. Generally, the raising of the soil level with humus-rich soil will not lessen the moisture content because water will seep up from the lower level by osmosis.

If you have an area close to a pond that you want to make into a bog but which currently drains too well, then you must dig down to the water table, remove the indigenous soil, and replace it with humus-rich, peaty soil. Seepage by osmosis from the water table is then likely to create the boggy condition you desire. Failing that, you will need to sink a trough or a bathtub and fill it with a humus-rich, moisture-retentive soil. Keep it moist by dripping water from a hose into the improved soil.

Fertilizing

To fertilize bog plants growing around the pond rim, it is best to use a granular fertilizer applied in spring. Make another application in autumn, after frost, with a high-phosphorus fertilizer. Bog plants usually have bulbous or fleshy roots that benefit from this nutrient.

Avoid using liquid or foliar fertilizers around water features, as these can easily drift into the water and may cause problems with the water's natural chemical balance, even poisoning fish.

Insert fertilizer tablets into the soil before submerging pots of waterlilies. Maintain a twice-weekly feeding schedule throughout the summer for lush and healthy plants.

Beneficial Aquatic Life

There are many pond scavengers that are an asset to water features since they do a remarkable job of cleaning. Hardy snails are good at vacuuming and trash pickup. They bury themselves in mud during winter. Stock your pond with one snail per 1 to 2 square feet (929 to 1,858 sq cm) of surface.

Tadpoles are the juvenile stage of frogs and toads. They hatch into great scavengers from jellylike egg masses that float near the surface of the water, eating all kinds of undesirable debris. Frogs eat

tremendous quantities of mosquito larvae, and although they will eat small fish they are unlikely to cause serious losses to a healthy fish population. Both tadpoles and frogs will go dormant in winter, lying motionless in the mud.

Bullfrogs are beneficial for water gardens because they eat harmful insect pests such as mosquito larvae. Their tadpoles also help keep the water clear.

Some Fish Facts

Goldfish and koi are the most popular ornamental fish. Goldfish are easier to raise than koi, since koi can grow bigger and are more sensitive to diseases. Yet some pond owners want fish they can eat. The most popular fish to eat are catfish, tilapia, bass, and trout. For trout, water temperature is extremely important, because the fish die when the temperature rises above 70°F (21°C). Where summers are hot, trout can be kept alive if the pool or pond has a cool, shaded grotto fed by an underground spring or a deep well into which they can swim and take refuge. Where pools are fed by municipal water supplies, you will need a chlorine remover to keep fish healthy. If water turns green from algae and will not clear, you may also need to apply a clarity chemical. Koi are especially prone to parasites and diseases, and a fish medication of sea salt may be needed. There are also medicated pellets for both koi and goldfish. Though fish will eat table scraps, especially bread crumbs, there are packaged fish foods containing a balanced formula of vitamins and minerals. Want to clear your garden of Japanese beetles? Show your children the fish-feeding frenzy that follows when you throw the fish a handful of Japanese beetles.

Pests and Diseases

Water plants are relatively free of common plant pests and diseases, although the leaves and flowers of some bog plants (like swamp hibiscus) can be prone to infestations of Japanese beetles and other chewing insects. However, it is best not to use any insecticides (even organic kinds) around water features, as they can be toxic to fish. The organic pesticide Rotenone is the best example of an organic insecticide that is lethal to fish.

If Japanese beetles and other similar insects do damage through chewing, handpick the populations and throw them into the water for the fish to eat. The feeding frenzy that follows is quite remarkable. By far the biggest damage to your plants is likely to come from animals and birds.

Deer

Deer will often step into a pool to eat succulent roots, waterlilies, and other aquatic plants. They have sharp hooves, which can puncture a flexible liner with ease. To avoid this problem, either fence deer out of the area or place some smooth stones or smooth gravel over the liner to cushion any intruding feet. Ponds are especially vulnerable to damage from deer in early spring and autumn.

Above: Japanese beetles can destroy plants around pond margins, especially hardy swamp hibiscus. If they fall into water fish gobble them up instantly! Below: Raccoons will enter shallow water in their search for fish and frogs, but they hate to swim.

Raccoons

Raccoons enjoy catching fish. They have hands like a monkey that grip easily, but they do not like to get completely wet. If a pond or pool has steep sides or high edging stones that overhang the water, fish can swim out of their reach.

Muskrats

If you see burrows that look like rabbit holes around the edges of your pond, or if holes appear in the lawn uphill or downhill from a pond, then chances are you have muskrats. These animals are herbivores that eat all kinds of aquatic vegetation, especially water-lilies. The biggest nuisance, however, is when they scratch through a liner and drain the pond. A cement apron at the outlet end of the pond can prevent muskrat damage. To prevent muskrats from eating waterlilies and to reduce the damage they inflict, you can place a high wire dome over the pots. But to rid your pond of them altogether requires trapping or shooting them where local ordinances allow.

Turtles

Turtles can do almost as much damage as muskrats, especially to waterlilies. You will know you have them when you see them basking on fallen logs or stones close to the water's edge. Except for snapping turtles, small turtles are mostly vegetarians. Don't bother them unless you are experiencing serious plant losses; a dome of wire mesh over waterlily pots can prevent serious damage. Small turtles can be netted for removal, but some snapping turtles can be as big as bathtubs and present a real danger to large fish, children, and pets. When snapping turtles feel threatened, they bite so strongly that only beheading them can release their grip. Turtles hibernate during winter, crawling into holes along stream and pond banks above the waterline.

Herons, Egrets, and Ospreys

Most gardeners are delighted to see these birds drawn to a pond or pool, but koi make an expensive meal for them, especially herons and egrets, which eat small fish as though they were bread crumbs. One form of protection is to provide a deck or a raft for the pond so that fish can shelter under it away from the prying beaks of these birds. Another preventive measure is to stretch black thread over the pond to interrupt their flight and walking movements.

Snakes

Snakes take easily to water and swim across ponds in search of fish, frogs, ducklings, and bird's eggs. Some water snakes (like the water moccasin, prevalent in southern states) have a poisonous bite and should be removed by netting them if they are spotted in a home pond or pool. At Cedaridge Farm we have a lot of nonpoisonous black water snakes, some as thick as my arm and up to 6 feet (1.8m) in length. Like muskrats, they can create holes that will drain a clay-lined pond, though they are unlikely to penetrate a liner. Snakes are not easy to trap, except by netting them with a long-handled net. In my experience the damage they do is minimal and I do not concern myself with them unless I find one lying close to a path where someone might be frightened by its presence. Snakes are cold-blooded and like to bask on sunny rocks between feedings. They go dormant at the first sign of frosty weather, hiding in holes and under loose stones.

Propagation

Of all the methods of propagation for aquatic plants, the easiest and most common is division. Most aquatic plants (including waterlilies and water irises) spread so prolifically by their roots that they need to be divided regularly. Many bog plants, such as Japanese primroses, are better to start from seed and will, in fact, readily self-seed if allowed to form seedpods. Not many aquatic plants are propagated from cuttings, but there are some good ornamental shrubs for boggy soils that can be, so it's useful to know the procedure. In the plant descriptions, information is given on the best way to propagate individual plant species. Listed here are the procedures for each method.

Seeds

Though many seed companies offer aquatic plant seeds in packets, you can often gather your own seeds by collecting seedpods as they ripen. Some good seed-producing plants include swamp hibiscus, all kinds of irises, bog primroses, cardinal flowers, marsh marigolds, and forget-me-nots. Seed-starting is especially desirable when you want to create large colonies of plants at a fraction of the cost of buying transplants.

Small fiber pots are ideal for raising seedlings like these water forget-me-nots. A peat-based potting soil suits most water plants. When growing water garden plants from seed, never allow the soil to dry out.

Begin by sowing the seeds in a seed tray filled with moist, peat-based potting soil, then cover the tray with a plastic freezer bag to maintain a moist microclimate. Store at room temperature in bright light (but not direct sunlight, which can overheat the soil and cause rapid dehydration). For finely seeded varieties like primroses, sow the seeds on the surface and lightly cover with just enough soil to anchor the seeds, or press the seeds into the soil surface. For large, easy-to-handle seeds like swamp hibiscus, cover completely with ¼ inch (6mm) of soil.

As soon as the seedlings are up, open the plastic cover and keep them growing with regular amounts of water and a mild liquid fertilizer. When seedlings are large enough to handle (½ inch [12mm] in height), transfer to individual peat or plastic pots and allow them to grow to a size that is easy to transplant—usually 2 to 3 inches (5 to 7.5cm) high.

Division

With many aquatic plants the division process is easy to see. Plants like water hyacinth and water lettuce throw off exact replicas of themselves so fast that they can quickly take over a large pond in one season. Simply pull up a clump and separate the divisions for transplanting. Irises are also easy to divide. Remove some from the pond and you'll see that the base is composed of bulbous roots, each with a crown of leaves. All it takes

Propagating Ferns

So many varieties of ferns relish moist soils and look exquisite around water features that it is impossible to have too many of them. The cheapest way to obtain a large number is to grow them from spores, which can be treated like tiny seeds to germinate and grow. Spores collected from a wild or cultivated plant will produce offspring identical to the parent. (Make sure to collect only spores, never the plants themselves.) Hybridization is possible by mixing spores from two dissimilar varieties in a peat-based growing medium.

To collect spores, take a leaf with brown blisters or dots on the underside. Examine the blisters carefully to see if they contain any raised, black, spore-bearing pinheads, indicating perfect ripeness. Tap the leaf onto some white paper to release the dustlike spores and sprinkle over a shallow dish filled with moist, sterile, peat-based potting soil. Insert the container into a plastic freezer bag to maintain a moist environment and leave for several months in bright light (but not direct sunlight). After several months the soil surface will be encased in a mosslike green covering from which fern fronds will later emerge. When the fern fronds are large enough to handle (1 inch [2.5cm] high), transfer to individual pots to reach transplant size (usually 4 inches [10cm]).

is a sharp knife to cut through the joints between them to make divisions for transplanting. Other plants, like waterlilies, are not so obvious because their root systems are completely covered. With tropical waterlilies, pull up a clump and wash away any soil to reveal small clumps crowned with leaves and connected by what look like umbilical cords. Sever the cords and plant each clump in a pot to size up. Hardy waterlilies have rhizomes with a crown of leaves and roots growing at intervals along the rhizome. Each section of rhizome with a crown and root system can be planted in a pot to size up.

Cuttings

Winterberry is a good example of a shrub that likes to grow in boggy soil. At Cedaridge Farm we have plants in places where the roots are permanently covered with water. Though it can be propagated from seeds found inside the red berries and also by dividing a vigorous clump, the easiest way to propagate it is by tip cuttings. This involves cutting a 6-inch (15cm) section of stem below a branch tip, stripping the leaves from the lower half, scraping the bark with a knife, and pushing the cut end into a pot with potting soil. The highest success rate is from branch tips taken in June or July before the new tip growth hardens. Place a group of cuttings in a seed tray, spaced 2 inches (5cm) apart. Also, it helps if the cut end is dipped in a powdery rooting hormone, available from garden centers. The rooting hormone encourages the cutting to root. Cover the cuttings with a plastic sheet to create a humid microclimate and place the seed tray in bright but not direct sunlight, since direct sunlight can scorch leaves and dry out soil rapidly.

Using a peat-perlite soil mix and misting to maintain a moist soil will result in a 90- to 100-percent success rate within 8 weeks. Examine the cuttings after 6 weeks to see if any rooting has begun. As soon as a healthy clump of roots is established, place the cuttings in individual pots to size up before transplanting.

Above: Flag irises are easily divided by uprooting a clump and cutting the roots apart. Simply replant the resulting divisions. Below: A rooted cutting of winterberry is ready to be transferred to an individual pot to size up before transplanting.

Water Garden Timetable

Each season brings with it changes that can affect the life cycle and health of your water garden. Here are tips on what to do at different times of year.

Spring

Inspect pool and pond sides for erosion and damage from ice. Also look for signs of muskrats, which are active in spring, making burrows along banks and eating vegetation. Raise hardy waterlilies from the bottom of the pool to within 12 inches (30cm) of the surface. Start filters. Check all electrical parts. Start fertilizing water plants. Move tropicals out of their winter quarters to their permanent positions. Visit aquatic garden centers for more plants. Evaluate the fish population. Stock the pond with more fish if necessary. Start seed or make divisions.

Summer

Check water levels for evaporation and add more water to pools and ponds whenever needed. If the level of your pool or pond drops to less than 12 inches (30cm), add more water or the fish will start to die from overheating and suffocation. If repairs are needed to a liner or dam, they are often easiest to do in the summer when the water level is naturally low. Keep filters clean. Maintain a fertilizing schedule, especially for waterlilies and lotus. Visit local botanical gardens and aquatic gardens to evaluate varieties of waterlilies. Herons, egrets, and ospreys can be extremely destructive to populations of fish in summer. Consider stretching fine threads across the pond surface to discourage their depredations. If a pond is becoming overgrown with weeds or algae, put on a pair of hip boots, step into the murky water, and pull the weeds out by hand. Toss it onto the bank where you can let it dry. Then delegate the dried mass to a compost pile.

Autumn

Clean ponds and pools. Scoop falling leaves from the surface each day with a long-handled net. Cover pools with tarps if necessary. Disconnect pumps and clear pipes so that freezing water does not damage essential parts. Drain filter and remove. Move hardy waterlilies off their pedestals down to the bottom of the pond below the ice line. Move tropicals indoors under glass or plastic into heated pools.

Winter

Stop feeding fish, since fish go dormant and food will sink to the bottom and contaminate the water. Begin feeding again only when the water temperature reaches 50°F (10°C). If pool and pond surfaces freeze, ensure that gasses from fermentation can escape through a hole. Study catalogs to order new equipment and plant supplies.

Water Garden Design

Opposite: This raised, circular pool creates an air of intimacy in a quiet corner of the garden.

The formality of this beautiful waterlily pool is softened somewhat by its rounded corners. A swing seat at the far end invites visitors to enjoy the view.

Pool Shapes

Many older formal pools are concrete-lined, but since they tend to be shallow and can be easily drained, repairs to cracks are easily made. However, most new formal pools rely on flexible PVC liners, since they are generally care-free. Formal pools can reflect formal surroundings—an Italian terrace garden, a French parterre, or a Persian reflecting pool is a perfect complement to a grand home. But a formal pool can also contrast with a natural environment. Indeed, a pool combining both formal and natural elements can be the most beautiful of all. One of the best designs in this style that I ever encountered was designed by Ohme Van Sweden & Associates for a suburban backyard. The side of the pool closest to the house had formal lines, with a flagstone deck providing a strong, straight edge to the pool, while the other side of the pool had an informal look, with bamboo, papyrus, and ornamental grasses arching out from a thickly planted edge.

Pool Shapes

Informal

The following four pond shapes are my favorites for an informal look.

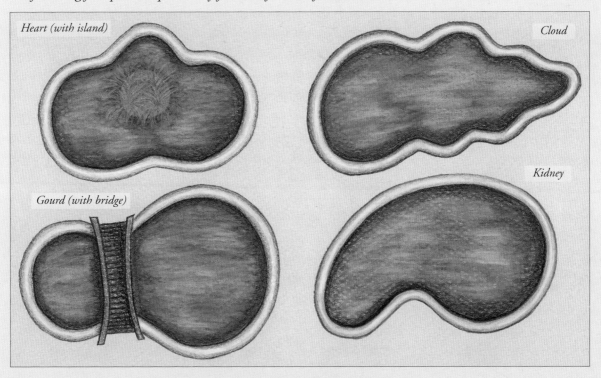

Formal

The following four pond designs show the most popular geometric shapes for a formal plan.

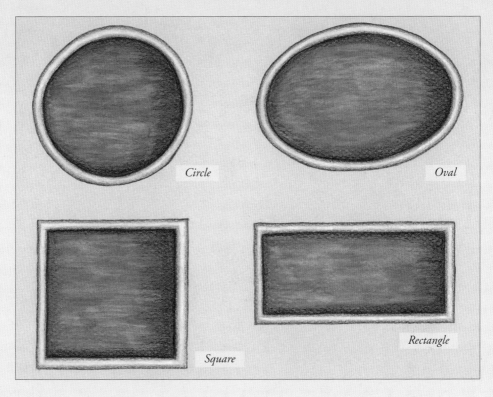

Natural Water Garden

This informal water garden is designed to look very natural. Thickets of winterberry provide food and cover for wildlife, while the fast-growing 'Heritage' river birches and dawn redwoods provide strong structural and skyline interest.

A Waterlily (*Nyphaea* spp.)
B Swamp hibiscus (*Hibiscus moscheutos*)
C 'Desdemona' bronze-leaf ragwort (*Ligularia dentata* 'Desdemona')
D Blue flag iris (*Iris versicolor*)
E Yellow flag iris (*Iris pseudacorus*)
F Ostrich fern (*Matteuccia struthiopteris*)
G 'Blue Angel' hosta (*Hosta* 'Blue Angel')
H Pickerel weed (*Pontederia cordata*)
I Japanese coltsfoot (*Petasites japonicus*)

J Cardinal flower (*Lobelia cardinalis*)
K Maiden grass (*Miscanthus sinensis*)
L Cattail (*Typha latifolia*)
M Bog primrose (*Primula* spp.)
N Forget-me-nots (*Myosotis scorpioides*)
O Goatsbeard (*Aruncus dioicus*)
P Dawn redwood (*Metasequoia glyptostroboides*)
Q 'Louisiana' hybrid iris (*Iris* 'Louisiana' hybrids)
R False spiraea, mixed colors (*Astilbe* × *arendsii*)

S 'Sum and Substance' hosta (*Hosta* 'Sum and Substance')
T Umbrella plant (*Peltiphyllum peltatum*)
U 'Superbum' snakeweed (*Polygonum bistorta* 'Superbum')
V 'Bowles Golden' grass (*Carex elata* 'Bowles Golden')
W Winterberry (*Ilex verticillata*)
X Horsechestnut plant (*Rodgersia aesculifolia*)
Y 'Heritage' river birch (*Betula nigra* 'Heritage')
Z Corkscrew rush (*Juncus effusus*)

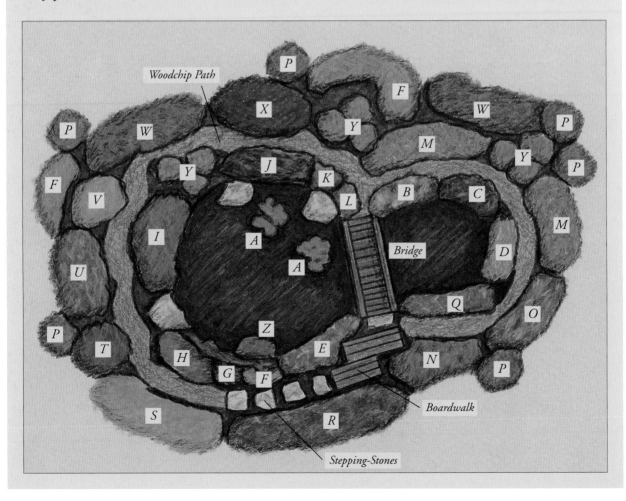

Reflections

Designing for beautiful reflections is as much a part of water gardening as choosing the right plants. My friend Hiroshi Makita, whose speciality is designing Zen gardens, likes to build water features, especially an arched bridge or an observation platform from which to view the reflection of the moon at dusk. Sometimes he must carve a vista from a neighboring tree canopy to create moon reflections; other times he must build the viewing structure high enough to see the moon reflected at the center of the pond. Makita takes into account existing structures, positioning water reflections to avoid unsightly buildings being reflected in the water.

Besides the moon, the most desirable reflections are those of trees and blue sky. Claude Monet, for example, designed his water garden to catch the nuances of color from changes in the sky, especially apricot sunrises and scarlet sunsets. He draped wisteria over arbors at the very edge of the water so that their blue blossoms would reflect where blue sky could not reach. Golden chain trees (*laburnum* × *vossii*) and trees with beautiful autumn foliage are also lovely reflected in water.

Large ponds may attract pairs of swans and colonies of geese. These birds can be a mixed blessing: while they are beautiful and may enrich the natural look of your pond, geese can create a mess around the margins of the pond while nesting swans can be aggressive.

Wildlife Ponds

All water features are attractive to wildlife, but to please waterfowl, songbirds, frogs, and native fish, be sure to site your wildlife pond in a woodland glade or amidst berry-bearing shrubs for protective cover and food. It is best if the water has sunlight streaming in from a break in the leaf canopy. Nearby boulders create a surface on which cold-blooded amphibians like frogs and turtles can sun themselves.

Waterfowl, like ducks and swans, cherish islands with shallow-rooted marginal plants like sedges and rushes for cover, because the water presents a protective barrier against many foraging animals. Also, waterfowl like to build nests among colonies of deep-rooted marginals, especially cattails. For songbirds such as wrens and chickadees, nesting boxes with small openings should be attached securely to old posts or tree trunks.

Some good berry-bearing shrubs to include around the perimeter of wildlife ponds are winterberry (*Ilex verticillata*), blueberry (*Vaccinium* spp.), blackberry (*Rubus* spp.), crabapple (*Malus* spp.), and wild strawberry (*Fragaria* spp.).

How to Create a Rainbow

At Swiss Pines Japanese garden near Philadelphia, garden designer Hiroshi Makita helped plan a water garden for the purpose of creating a double rainbow. He achieved this by installing a bamboo pipe that sends a water jet from high above a path to the boulders far below. Before the jet of water reaches the boulders it has already started to separate into droplets. When the spray of water hits the boulders, these droplets splinter into the kind of billowing, fine mist you sometimes see at the base of a waterfall. On a sunny day sunlight shines through the mist like a prism, creating the double rainbow. A small amount of mist creates a single rainbow while a large amount results in a double.

Stonework Beside a Stream and Waterfall

When creating a waterfall and a rocky stream, there are different types of stones used for different purposes. Below are the most important kinds and their proper names.

A   Mirror stone—a smooth, flat stone behind the falls

B   Flanking stones—large stones to frame the falls

C   Base stones—for foundation support

D   Water-dividing stone—can be used as a stepping-stone

E   Wave-dividing stone—can be used as a stepping-stone

F   Edging stones—to retain the stream bank

G   Fill stones—to support the falls

H   Observation stone—for admiring the view

I   Stepping-stones—for access to an observation stone

Cascades

The best way to introduce water to a pool or pond is through a waterfall or cascade. In formal gardens the cascade itself can be formal—a solid sheet of water that presents a wide, flat flow like a mirror or an arching stream that shoots water out in a jet. In informal gardens the waterfall can flow over a group of boulders, splashing musically from left to right as rocks interrupt the flow. It is crucial that any stones or boulders used in a cascade, whether placed formally or informally, be securely seated—preferably in concrete, with a flexible liner below the concrete so that it doesn't matter if the concrete cracks.

If you plan to imitate a waterfall from another garden or from the wild and want to know the volume of water you'll need to recirculate, place a 5-gallon (19L) bucket under the flow and time how long it takes for the bucket to fill. If it takes a minute to fill, then the flow is 5 gallons (19L) per minute. Your local aquatic center can then recommend a recirculating pump of the appropriate size. For more complicated waterfalls and cascades, however, it's safest to hire an experienced professional to do the calculation and installation.

This man-made waterfall in the Japanese tradition features a gentle cascade with boulders that break the water into "silver threads."

Waterfall Styles

Below are examples of waterfalls often used in gardens. Placement of stones creates the different effects, from a single silvery thread to a wide cascade.

Silver Thread　　　　*Falling Cloth*　　　　*Multi Threads*

Broken Cloth　　　　*Broken Falls*　　　　*Stepped Falls*

When water flow is low this waterfall features strands of water, known as silver threads; when flow is heavy the water forms a solid sheet, called a falling cloth. Note the massive flanking stones that make this manmade waterfall so impressive.

Bog Gardens

The marshy ground around this pond supports a diversity of flowering and foliage plants, including ferns and irises.

Do not confuse bog plants with aquatic plants, since bog plants—like ostrich ferns and astilbes—generally do not survive with their roots permanently covered with water. If you do not already have a swampy area on your property in which to plant a bog garden, you can create one by seeping water from a hose into a peat-based soil so that the site is kept constantly moist but not flooded.

Many homes have existing wetlands with large areas of moist soil in which to create a marshlike habitat, but you can also create a bog garden along a stream or in a small area bordering a pond. I have even seen bog gardens in sunken bathtubs, with the soil in the bathtub planted with beautiful pitcher plants and kept moist by a dripping faucet. The plug-hole in the tub provided sufficient drainage.

At Cedaridge Farm we have a bog garden that surrounds an old ash tree. A path of pine needles alternates between high ground and swampy soil, crossing the low areas by means of a boardwalk at the start of the path and by stepping-stones at the end. On the border of the bog garden, we have introduced groves of two fast-growing bog-loving trees: *Betula nigra* 'Heritage', a variety of river birch with honey-colored bark, and *Metasequoia glyptostroboides,* the dawn redwood. Both relish moist soil and grow at the rate of 5 feet (1.5m) a year. They are dramatic when combined because the light coloration of the birches contrasts so well with the dark, feathery green leaves of the dawn redwoods.

Japanese Water Gardens

Small millstones serve as stepping-stones along a stream planted with water hyacinths in this small-space Japanese water garden.

I t is not necessary to travel to Japan to study the concept of traditional Japanese gardens, since many fine examples exist in North America (especially in California and the Pacific Northwest). There are also many books available explaining the principles of Japanese garden design.

In many locations, traditional Japanese structures like tea houses, stone towers, lanterns, and expanses of raked gravel can look a little incongruous. But gardens with a traditional Japanese balance of water, evergreens, and boulders that symbolize an imagined natural landscape of weather-worn elements looks appealing anywhere.

Tropical Water Gardens

A tropical water garden designed by world-famous landscape architect, the late Roberto Burle Marx, features the giant Amazon waterlily.

You don't need to live in a tropical or semitropical climate to enjoy exotic water plants that look as though they would be at home in the Amazon rain forest. Tropical water gardens can be created indoors in the corner of sunrooms and conservatories. They can also be made for mostly outdoor summer enjoyment, with the plants in pots

moved indoors during freezing months. Even large tropical plants, like Australian tree ferns and banana trees, can be grown in pots and overwintered indoors in a heated room that provides bright filtered light.

Tropical water gardens need more than tall tropical trees to look their best. Consideration should be given to planting flowering orchids and bromeliads around the margin. Also spectacular are exotic vines like philodendron overhanging the pool and the bananalike leaves of 'Pretoria' canna emerging from the water. Other cherished plants for tropical water gardens are elephant's ear (*Colocasia esculenta*) and the extra-large Amazon waterlily (*Victoria amazonica*), with pads that can exceed 10 feet (3m) in width and a huge, white, star-shaped flower that smells like a pineapple.

Canals, Millraces, Channels, and Rills

These artificial water features are variations on the same theme. A canal is a long, rectangular, artificial watercourse. A canal that encircles a building is called a moat.

A millrace is a narrow corridor (usually emanating from a nearby stream or river) along which water flows quickly by force of gravity to turn a millwheel or feed a pond. The water flow into the millrace is usually controlled by a sluice gate, which can be opened and closed to regulate the volume.

A channel is a narrow, straight water passage between two water features. It usually connects a fountain at one end to a formal pool at the other. Channels are a popular feature of Persian- and Indian-style water gardens. A rill is similar to a channel, but it snakes its way through a natural environment, connecting two water features such as a natural spring and a pond. An advantage of channels and rills is that they can be stepped over easily.

The edges of all these water features can be embellished with marginals and bog plants and crisscrossed with either stepping-stones or low footbridges.

This pair of rills snakes through a boggy area, ready to be planted with moisture-loving Japanese primroses.

Steps and Stepping-Stones

These stepping-stones have pebbles cemented to the treads to provide a solid, nonslip surface. Still, good balance is needed to negotiate this path!

S teps are useful for climbing alongside waterfalls to an overlook or observation platform, while stepping-stones are suitable for crossing sections of boggy soil or water as an alternative to a boardwalk or bridge. Steps have risers (the vertical part) and treads (the horizontal part). It is best to make the steps of stone, since wooden steps (unless made from tree trunks) rarely look natural. For maximum comfort and safety, the total measurement of two risers and one tread should equal 26 to 27 inches (65 to 67.5cm). Also, the maximum riser height should not exceed 6½ inches (16.5cm), and the minimum tread depth should be 11 inches (27.5cm). If the ascent is steep, the steps should have a handrail for safety.

Stepping-stones are usually made from flat, irregular-shaped boulders, from square sections of flagstone, or from round millstones. It is crucial that the stones are firmly seated on pedestals of concrete sunk into the stream bottom and supported on a collar of concrete so that they do not wobble and pitch visitors into the water. Since stepping-stones can be slippery after rain or when soaked in spray from a waterfall, the surface should be scored to make it nonslippery.

Stepping-Stone Paths

Before placing stepping-stones in a stream, lay them out on land and walk over them to ensure that the distance between them is not too great. Make sure that the size of the stones can accommodate an easy number of steps without having to shuffle the feet. Each stone ideally should allow for one, two, or three comfortable strides, as shown in the diagram below. Never use stepping-stones across vast sections of water. For more than 12 feet (3.6m), consider instead installing a boardwalk or a zigzag bridge.

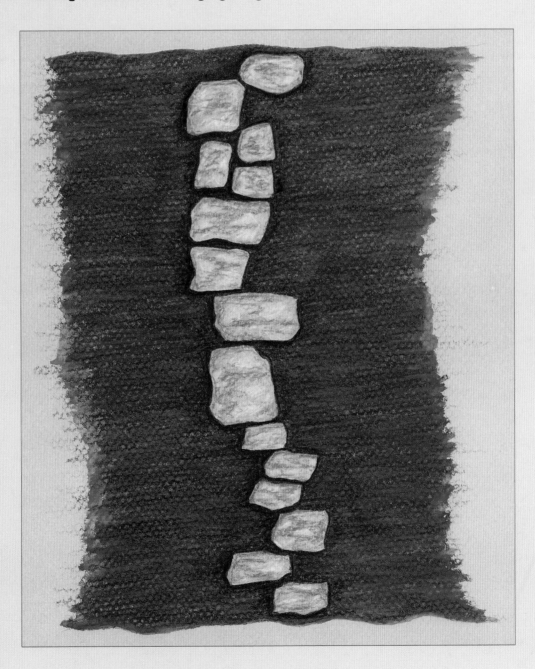

Pebbles and Stones

One of Japan's most beautiful sights is a wide, curving expanse of beach created entirely from blue-black stones the size of goose eggs at the Sento Imperial Palace Garden in Kyoto. Gathered by hand from a special beach, each stone was wrapped in rice paper and loaded onto an ox cart for the journey to the garden. Likewise, you can scour local quarries, streamsides, and beaches for beautiful pebbles and stones to add texture and natural beauty to your pools and ponds. When you find a stone coated with lichens, algae, or moss, carefully wrap it in burlap for its journey to the garden so that the covering survives to give your water garden a look of maturity.

A whimsical snail fountain spouts water over its head. Fountains help to oxygenate water for a healthy fish population.

Fountains

In water garden design, if a waterfall is the ace in the deck of elements we play with and waterlilies are king, then a fountain surely must be the queen. A fountain allows us to introduce the sight and sound of gushing water to an area where it is difficult to have a waterfall. It is a favored ornament for formal water gardens, because a particular style of fountain can immediately establish a garden's theme. For example, a baroque stone fountain adds Italian flair, an ornate metal fountain

Wall-Mounted Fountains

A simple way to introduce the sound of splashing water to a garden—especially a courtyard, where sound can echo from nearby walls—is to use a wall-mounted fountain. Popular designs available from garden centers include lion, Medusa, and dolphin heads with matching bowls to catch the water. A small, silent pump set in the base of the bowl can recirculate the water. Aquatic centers usually have several designs on display so that you can judge their sound qualities. All components can be purchased in a kit for easy installation.

suggests a French or Victorian flavor, and a low, bubbling fountain can introduce a modern theme. Fountains have the additional benefit of oxygenating water, which keeps fish healthy.

Remember that in nature the upward force of water is seen only rarely among blow-holes along rocky coasts and geysers in areas with volcanic activity, so they don't fit easily into natural water garden designs. But fountains are marvelous devices for adding a musical accent to formal spaces like city courtyards and atriums.

Fountains, of course, require pumps, and these can be obtained through aquatic centers in consultation with an expert.

Spillways

A spillway is a stone or wooden dam that holds back water along a stream to form a pond. There is generally a depression in the center serving as an overflow. Spillways were popular in colonial days, but today local ordinances

This spillway is used to divert water along a millrace—further downstream the water turns a heavy waterwheel.

may restrict their height and the size of the pond they can form. They are prone to damage and erosion along the sides unless properly installed but make a truly beautiful water feature because stepping-stones and short bridge spans can cross the gap that forms the overflow.

Small spillways can be created along streams to produce a series of water steps. When a series of stone spillways holds back the water into pools, then any gaps to the left, right, or middle can spill water in a visually appealing pattern of falls.

Container Water Gardens

Containers have both a decorative and a utilitarian function in the water garden. Those used beneath the water to confine aquatic plants don't need to be decorative. Indeed, inexpensive plastic ones work fine. But aquatic plants can also be grown in containers to add color and interest on decks and patios. An aboveground, self-contained unit not only needs to be decorative, it usually looks best when it contains a mixture of aquatic plants to create a miniature water garden.

A small self-contained water garden in a tub features an assortment of plants growing in submerged pots.

Submerged Containers

Even if your pool or pond is large, it is best to restrict plants to containers, especially inexpensive, lightweight, and durable plastic pots. Containerized plants are easier to move and fertilize, and containers will confine the vigorous spreading roots of even the most aggressive plants. When tropicals are used, the plants can be saved from year to year when planted in containers. Simply lift the pots out of the water and store them indoors under glass or plastic in a heated holding tank.

Many aquatic plants like water lettuce and hardy waterlilies have shallow, spreading root systems, so pan-shaped containers with 8 inches (20cm) of soil depth are ideal. Others, like cattails and lotuses, benefit from deeper, tub-shaped pots with a minimum 10-gallon (38L) capacity for a decent display. Make sure that the pots rest on a sturdy pedestal of some kind, such as a heavy upturned pot or a metal crate. If you want the pot to rest on the bottom, put a heavy piece of flagstone or tile beneath it. Mud bottoms can be unstable and can tip the pot during wind and water movement. Pots should have no drainage holes, since probing roots can grow through and escape into the pond to become a nuisance. A liner of folded newspaper or a strip of tar paper can be used to block a drainage hole.

Note that a layer of pebbles on top of the soil helps to prevent potting soil from washing away when submerged in a pot.

For containers, a good soil mix is four parts garden topsoil or slightly clay soil mixed with one part compost, well-decomposed manure, or peat. For every 5 gallons (19L) of soil, add ½ cup (125g) of granular all-purpose fertilizer (10-10-10). Fill the bottom half of the container with soil mix before placing the plant in the pot. Then fill tubs to within 2 inches (5cm) of the top, firm the soil around plants, and add a l-inch (2.5cm) layer of gravel to weigh down the soil so that it doesn't work loose and drift away.

Most flowering water plants, like waterlilies and lotuses, are heavy feeders and require fertilizing regularly. Use aquatic fertilizers in pill form for best results. These are high in phosphorus and should be pushed down several inches into the pot, where they can dissolve and be absorbed by the plant's roots. For rates of application read the label, since different brands have different formulations. The typical dosage is one pill every two weeks from spring through summer.

Aboveground Containers

It's fun to create a self-contained water garden. Even small pots can be planted to create a microecosystem that can sustain fish and maintain clear water. The bigger the container, however, the more creative you can be. Some good containers to consider include metal cauldrons, bathtubs, whiskey half-barrels, and terra-cotta tubs. Whiskey half-barrels are such a popular choice that aquatic centers offer circular rigid liners that fit right into the barrel to prevent rot.

Aboveground water gardens should not have any soil in the bottom. All plants should be grown in submerged containers with stacked bricks used to maintain the different depths needed for each type of plant. The rules for balanced planting in ponds also apply to aboveground containers, which need both floating and oxygenating plants to purify the water and support a population of fish. Don't overlook the possibility of using a pump to create a miniature waterfall or a spinning fountain. You may also position dry-land plants around the rim to soften hard lines. Japanese maples, for example, spread their feathery leaves over the lip of the container and into the water.

The Best Plants for
Water Gardens

Opposite: Tall Joe-Pye weed, ostrich ferns, and pink false spiraea colonize the edges of a pond.

BRADFORD WG LIBRARY
100 HOLLAND COURT, BOX 130
BRADFORD, ONT. L3Z 2A7

The following selection of plants suitable for water gardens represents a diverse range of uses. Floating and submerged plants, like waterlilies, that like their roots covered with water, and bog plants, which like the moist soil of low-lying areas along ponds and streams, are among

A small rock garden at Cedaridge Farm features a waterlily pool; a vine-covered guest cottage makes a perfect backdrop for the garden scene.

those included. This is not an all-inclusive survey of every plant regarded as aquatic or bog-loving, but it is a good selection of the flowering kinds and also of those that present excellent foliage effects.

In choosing the photographs I have tried to show overall views of the plants rather than close-ups and, in particular, recommended uses of the plants. Many of these scenes are from plantings at my home, Cedaridge Farm. Heights, where given, are approximate. Height may vary according to light intensity, soil fertility, and other growth factors. Where a choice variety is available, it is highlighted in the text. For recommended sources of these and other water plants, see the source list on page 116.

Acorus calamus 'Variegatus'

(*sweet flag*)

In outward appearance this hardy, evergreen, bog-loving plant resembles a clump of irises, with arching, sword-shaped leaves emanating from a colony of irislike rhizomes. The chopped rhizomes are sweetly fragrant and are valued by herbalists as a fixative for potpourris and a substitute for orris root, to which some people are allergic. At Cedaridge Farm we have a large colony bordering a path that runs through our marsh garden. It's delightful to walk along the path, pick a leaf, and offer it to a visitor to smell the pleasant aroma.

Sweet flag's flowers are inconspicuous, each composed of a small arumlike flower sheath and a powdery column that appears in spring. The decorative quality of the leaves—especially in the golden-and-green cultivar, 'Variegatus'—makes it an attractive marginal or bog-loving foliage accent.

Plants grow to 18 inches (45cm) high and look good individually in submerged pots or massed as an edging along ponds in contrast with other foliage plants like ferns and hostas. There are several miniature varieties with different forms of variegation, including silver-leaf forms popular in Japanese gardens for planting between cracks in flagstone. A related species, *A. gramineus*, also has many miniature, variegated cultivars. All are easily propagated by division of the rhizomes.

The moisture-loving sweet flag in the foreground contrasts with flowering fountain grass, which likes dry soil.

Lime green flower clusters of lady's mantle spill decoratively over a rock ledge into a pool.

Alchemilla mollis
(l a d y ' s   m a n t l e)

Valued for its beautiful, silver-green, ivylike leaves, this bog-loving perennial has the added bonus of growing billowing clusters of lime green flowers in spring and thriving in sun or light shade. In the early morning, the velvetlike leaves collect beads of dew and concentrate them in a sparkling water droplet at every leaf center. At Cedaridge Farm we use lady's mantle to edge the pond and as part of green foliage gardens planted along woodland paths.

The mound-shaped plants grow to 2 feet (60cm) high and relish a humus-rich soil, especially in pockets of soil among boulders and flagstones where the flowers can cascade out and down to touch the water. Plants look very attractive planted among ferns and hostas. Planted as a groundcover, lady's mantle makes a wonderful transition between taller plants like swamp hibiscus and astilbe and plants growing in the water. Propagate by division after flowering.

Arum italicum 'Pictum'
(I t a l i a n   a r u m)

Related to Jack-in-the-pulpit (*Arisaema triphyllum*), this native of Mediterranean regions is not used nearly enough in water gardens. It passes through three phases of interest so its effects are particularly long-lasting. Italian arum first delights with decorative arrow-shaped leaves that persist through winter, then with hooded lime green flower spathes that appear in spring, and finally with the ripening of its red pokerlike seed clusters, which occur in late summer. The cultivar 'Pictum' is especially desirable because of its beautiful white-and-green marbled foliage.

Many other arums are valuable in bog gardens, both for their interesting hooded flowers and their unique trifoliate leaves. Two of my favorites are the large purple-spathed *Dracunculus vulgaris* and smaller-flowered *Arisaema sikokianum*, which features a prominent white spadix and striped hood.

Italian arum grows 2 feet (60cm) high, thrives in sun or shade, and prefers a humus-rich, boggy soil. Use among hostas and ferns for an attractive plant partnership. Propagate by seed or by division. Handle with care, because all parts are considered toxic.

Right: Italian arum's berry clusters form in late summer. Below: Goatsbeard displays its striking white flower plumes.

Aruncus dioicus

(*g o a t s b e a r d*)

This hardy perennial resembles a giant form of white-flowering *Astilbe* but has a more commanding presence in the landscape, growing taller, spreading thicker, and producing larger flowers. The dark green leaves are composed of leaflets with a feathery appearance. The loose, pointed flower clusters can be more than 18 inches (45cm) long and just as wide. Plants grow to 5 feet (1.5m) high, prefer a humus-rich, boggy soil, and tolerate light to medium shade.

Goatsbeard is especially good to use in company with other large waterside plants, such as Chilean rhubarb, Japanese coltsfoot, yellow flag irises, and blue hostas. At Cedaridge Farm we plant it between colonies of false spiraea and blue flag irises. Propagation is by division after flowering.

Variegated giant reed grows in a submerged pot, filling out a water garden design that highlights decorative foliage.

Arundo donax 'Variegata'
(giant reed)

This marvelous, hardy, grasslike perennial is appropriate wherever a strong highlight is needed for bridging the gap between low-growing waterside plants and tall surrounding trees. The leaves are handsomely marked with white and green longitudinal stripes. The plant emerges from winter dormancy in early spring and quickly grows to 10 feet (3m) or more. The tall, towering stems flower in autumn with silky gray flower plumes.

Use the variegated giant reed with other large grasslike plants, such as pampas plume and maiden grass, and giant marginals such as Japanese coltsfoot, Chilean rhubarb, and Joe-Pye weed. We have a particularly beautiful streamside planting that contrasts the ribbonlike leaves of giant reed with the slender sparkling foliage of variegated zebra grass (*Miscanthus sinensis* 'Zebrinus'). Provide the roots with a humus-rich, boggy soil. Propagate by division in spring or summer.

Astilbe x arendsii
(false spiraea)

The late Georg Arends, a German plant breeder, pioneered the breeding of many *Astilbe* hybrids, producing some spectacular free-flowering varieties in shades of red, pink, purple, and white. They grow well in full sun but are also invaluable for lightly shaded, humus-rich, boggy soils. I like to plant them in drifts of separate colors around the pond and beside our stream, especially within view of our arched bridge. Some notable cultivars include 'Fanal' (dark red),

'Deutchland' (white), and 'Rheinland' (a shimmering deep pink). The feathery flower heads make beautiful arrangements, both fresh and dried.

Plants grow to 3 feet (90cm) high, display deeply serrated leaflets, and are capable of establishing large colonies besides ponds and streams. They are especially attractive in company with hostas, ostrich ferns, and ligularia. Propagate by division.

Feathery false spiraea contrast well with the spiky leaves of flag irises and the rounded leaves of waterlilies.

Betula nigra 'Heritage'

(*'Heritage' birch*)

If ever a plant could be called a wonder tree, this is it. Though river birch grow wild throughout North America, they are generally unimpressive trees with rough, dark brown bark. 'Heritage' is a special mutation discovered in a St. Louis garden by nurseryman Earl Cully. It is distinctive for its exfoliating honey-colored bark and its ability to tolerate a wide range of soils, including boggy soil. At Cedaridge Farm we have a grove of twenty-five heritage birches planted along a stream and clumps of three to seven strategically planted around our pond. Under some of them we planted giant Japanese coltsfoot for a dramatic plant partnership.

Even more beautiful than the New England white birch, 'Heritage' is disease-resistant and grows at the rate of 5 feet (1.5m) a year, quickly becoming a handsome, pyramid-shaped shade tree. Yellow flowers called catkins occur in spring, followed by mint green serrated leaves that turn golden yellow in autumn. The bark remains decorative all through winter.

Above: 'Heritage' birch remains ornamental through winter because of its attractive bark. Below: Marsh marigolds prosper along a stream bank.

Trees grow to 60 feet (18m) high and should be planted at least 6 feet (1.8m) apart. Propagation is by tip cuttings taken in spring. Bareroot transplants are available from mail-order sources, and balled trees can be obtained from tree nurseries. Spring planting is preferred over autumn.

Caltha palustris

(*marsh marigold*)

These hardy perennials resemble large buttercups and prefer to be planted in very wet soil or shallow water. They flower early, at the same time as daffodils, making mounded clumps of lustrous, heart-shaped green leaves. The shimmering yellow cup-shaped flowers open flat in the sun. A double-flowered form, 'Flore Pleno', is extremely free-flowering. On my farm, I planted several marsh marigolds that I found growing in a ditch, and these have seeded themselves freely along the stream.

Plants are easily propagated by division after flowering and from seed. They are good companions to Japanese primroses, forget-me-nots, yellow skunk cabbage, and ostrich ferns. Individually, they work well in pots and submerged as marginal plants for both formal and informal pools.

Canna × generalis 'Pretoria'

(*striped canna*)

There are two kinds of canna popular for water gardens—hybrids like 'Pretoria' that prefer boggy soil and water canna hybrids that thrive with their roots permanently submerged in water. The best of the water cannas are the 'Longwood' hybrids, with their broad, spear-shaped leaves and yellow, red, or pink flowers.

The striped leaves of 'Pretoria' canna, backlit by the sun, enliven a poolside planting in summer.

Among regular cannas, the variety 'Pretoria' stands above the rest because of its large bananalike leaves that are striped like a tiger. In fact, another name for it is 'Bengal Tiger'. The flowers are orange and appear late in the season, but the ornamental value of the leaves is evident as soon as the bulb sprouts in spring and the effect lasts until autumn frost.

Cannas are tender plants that grow up to 6 feet (1.8m) tall. They can be overwintered by lifting the bulbs, cleaning them of soil, and storing them in a dry, dark, frost-free place. 'Pretoria' is particularly effective massed as a pondside planting and mixed with ornamental grasses such as maiden grass. At Cedaridge Farm we use it as a background highlight for mixed container plantings. Propagate by bulb division.

Carex elata ⌐'Bowles Golden'

(B o w l e s   g o l d e n   g r a s s)

Contrasting beautifully with both statuary and natural stone, a clump of 'Bowles Golden' grass decorates a small waterlily pool at Cedaridge Farm.

Though it looks like a grass, this is actually a hardy perennial sedge that is widely distributed throughout the northern hemisphere, across North America, Europe, and Asia. I've found that this is the best of many ornamental grasses for boggy soil. It forms a fountainlike clump of slender arching leaves, almost as yellow as a daffodil in light shade. At Cedaridge Farm we use it everywhere—singly in company with blue forget-me-nots and massed along our stream bank with blue hostas and ostrich ferns. We also have a pot of it submerged in shallow water in one of our rock garden pools, where it casts a magnificent reflection.

Plants grow to 2 feet (60cm) high and equally wide, and produce inconspicuous brown flower plumes in spring. They prefer a humus-rich, moist soil and tolerate both sun and shade. Propagate by division in spring. Some other grasslike bog plants to consider as companion plantings to 'Bowles Golden' are snowy woodrush (*Luzula nivea*), 'Picta' ribbon grass (*Phalaris arundinacea*), switch grass (*Panicum virgatum*), rushes (*Juncus*), and cotton grass (*Eriophorum latifolium*).

Colocasia esculenta

(e l e p h a n t ' s   e a r)

Also known as green taro, this tropical plant has leaves that can measure 5 feet (1.5m) long, depending on the size of the bulb from which it grows. In the Polynesian islands, the bulbs are pounded into a flour that forms the basis of poi, a food staple. Though the plants are sensitive to frost damage, the bulbs can be easily lifted after the tops have died down and should be stored in a dry, dark, frost-free place to overwinter. The bulbs should be planted in containers about six weeks before the last frost date, then moved outdoors after frost danger. The pots can be submerged in shallow water or in boggy soil beside ponds and streams.

Elephant's ear grows up to 10 feet (3m) high. It helps create a tropical accent for water gardens and looks good with cannas, swamp hibiscus, Egyptian papyrus, and tropical waterlilies. It grows well in full sun and light shade. The flowers are inconspicuous—a pale hooded sheath with a yellow spadix rarely produced in northern climates.

The dramatic heart-shaped leaves of elephant's ears add a tropical accent to water gardens. Overwinter the bulbs indoors.

Cyperus alternifolius

(*umbrella palm*)

Not a true palm, this relative of the Egyptian papyrus plant (*C. papyrus*) is not as tall, so it is more suitable for small ponds and pools. For large ponds, use the Egyptian papyrus in company with tall water plants like elephant's ear and cannas. Papyrus requires growing conditions identical to those of the umbrella palm.

The umbrella palm is an attractive foliage plant that thrives with its roots submerged in water. Clumps of slender, erect flower stems grow to 3 feet (90cm) high, and are topped by a whorl of radiating needlelike leaves that make a starburst pattern similar to the spokes of an umbrella. Grow it in pots or in moist, humus-rich soil saturated with water. Good companion plants include tropical waterlilies, 'Bowles Golden' grass, and cannas. Since the umbrella palm is frost-tender, it must be overwintered under cover in a heated storage tank. Propagate by division.

Above: At the St. Louis Botanical Garden, varieties of umbrella palm stand tall and luxuriant in a formal raised pool divided into two square water basins. Below: A colony of cobra lilies shows their interesting hoods.

Darlingtonia californica

(*cobra lily*)

Challenging is the word for this amazing native aquatic wildflower that colonizes sphagnum bogs in northern California and coastal Oregon. If you can provide it with boggy soil and a mild winter, it is worth a try. The plant lures insects, attracted by its odor, into a hooded funnel-shaped trap formed from fused leaves. Having entered the trap, the insects follow a series of downward pointing hairs to a digestive liquid in which they perish and dissolve, to be absorbed by the plant as a nutrient. The entrance to the hood has a pair of wavy leaf parts resembling the forked tongue of a snake. In home gardens they are best confined to a pot, sunk into boggy soil, and overwintered indoors during freezing weather. In spring the plants produce translucent veined hoods and curious yellow or purple nodding flowers on stems 3 to 4 feet (90 to 120cm) high.

Collecting these plants from the wild is forbidden, since they are endangered. Propagation is mostly by seed. Nursery-grown transplants are available from aquatic plant nurseries and mail-order sources.

A popular floating plant, water hyacinth bloom happily all summer but need protection from frost.

Eichhornia crassipes
(*water hyacinth*)

Be aware that in southern states this floating plant is considered a noxious weed. Native to South America, its capacity for spreading is so great that huge colonies have choked lakes, canals, and waterways, particularly in the Gulf states. In Florida manatees eat them, but there aren't enough manatees to keep the plants under control. In northern gardens, however, the water hyacinth is an attractive plant with bulbous stems that allow it to float. It has rounded green leaves and blue flowers, which form a column up to 4 inches (10cm) long like a Dutch hyacinth. Feathery roots hang down and take nutrients from the water. These roots do not need to be anchored in soil. Use in company with other floating plants such as water clover and mosaic plant.

Plants grow to 12 inches (30cm) high and spread rapidly. They are killed by frost and in northern gardens must be overwintered in a heated holding tank. Flowering occurs in summer. Propagation is by division.

Equisetum hyemale

(*horsetail*)

Unless this hardy perennial is confined to a pot it will escape and spread aggressively into other parts of the garden. In small clumps it is a beautiful bog plant with strong architectural lines. Its stems are slender, round, pointed like asparagus spears, and notched with dark bands like bamboo. The tubular stems are pointed and topped with a spore-bearing cone. Good companion plants include umbrella palms, Japanese irises, and arrowheads.

Plants grow to 2 feet (60cm) tall, though there is a giant variety, 'Robustum', which can exceed 5 feet (1.5m) in height. Give them full sun and boggy soil. Grown in a pot, the plants can be submerged 6 inches (15cm). Make sure the pot has its drainage hole closed; otherwise, the rhizomes will poke through and escape to become invasive. Propagate by dividing the rhizomes.

Because horsetails can be invasive it is usually best to confine their roots to a submerged pot. Or plant them where natural obstacles—such as boulders or shrubs—will control them.

Eupatorium purpureum

(*Joe-Pye weed*)

Native to damp meadows of the northeastern United States, these hardy perennials are tolerant of boggy soil. They present a dramatic background highlight for ponds and streams, particularly when cultivated with other tall-growing plants like giant reed, maiden grass, and Japanese coltsfoot. They have erect stems up to 6 feet (1.8m) tall, topped by huge, smoky pink flower clusters up to 18 inches (45cm) across. Flowering in summer, plants form clumps and may need staking to keep the stems erect. Plants prefer full sun and a humus-rich, moist soil.

'Gateway' is an especially desirable cultivar of Joe-Pye weed because of its extra-large flowers and deep pink coloration. Use sparsely in colonies around ponds and pools and along stream banks. The flowers are highly attractive to swallowtail butterflies. The plants are easily propagated by division.

Joe-Pye weed is a native North American wildflower that thrives in moist meadows and along stream banks, flowering in summer.

Gunnera manicata
(Chilean rhubarb)

If there is a larger-leafed perennial for boggy soil I have yet to see it. A familiar sight in European water gardens, especially at the edge of ponds, Chilean rhubarb is not reliably hardy on the East Coast north of Washington, D.C. On the West Coast it thrives from San Diego to Vancouver, Canada. The individual leaves can grow to 9 feet (2.7m) across and equally as long. They are covered with spines and have sharply serrated edges like a rhubarb leaf. A brown, cone-shaped flower appears in spring, often before the leaves are fully unfurled. There is a similar variety, *G. chilensis*, that is slightly hardier and only slightly smaller-flowered, but both need winter protection wherever the ground freezes. This can be provided by planting the roots in a submerged bottomless box and covering them in winter with glass or plastic. You can also grow the plants in large tubs of 10- to 25-gallon (38 to 95L) capacity and sunk in soil in a cold frame or plastic tunnel to overwinter.

Use Chilean rhubarb sparingly as a dramatic pondside accent in sun or light shade. The humus-rich soil must be deep, fertile, and boggy. Propagation is by division. It is difficult to find plants that look good with this monster, but giant hogweed and Japanese coltsfoot work well. It also looks wonderful surrounded by Japanese primroses.

Chilean rhubarb makes a dramatic accent plant, but its roots are sensitive to hard, prolonged freezes.

Heracleum mantegazzianum

(giant hogweed)

The lacy white flowers of giant hogweed are pretty to look at—but don't touch the sap that oozes from its cut stems, as this can cause serious skin irritation.

First, a warning: this very tall, hardy perennial can cause severe dermatitis and itching if the sap from its huge leaves or thick hollow stems touches bare skin. It has, however, a sculptural beauty with its broad, indented rhubarblike leaves, tall stems up to 10 feet (3m) high, and white flower clusters up to 2 feet (60cm) across. The whole plant resembles a gigantic Queen Anne's lace.

Hogweed is a good companion for other giant-size perennials such as giant reed, Chilean rhubarb, and Japanese coltsfoot. Plants prefer a humus-rich, boggy soil in sun or partial shade. They are easily propagated by seed and by division, but handle the division with gloves.

Hibiscus moscheutos

(swamp hibiscus)

The wild species is a beautiful, flowering, hardy perennial native to northeastern and midwestern swamps. It has been hybridized to create large-flowered varieties such as 'Southern Belle' and 'Disco Belle'. At Cedaridge Farm we have the wild species planted in our marsh garden and the hybrids planted around our pond. Though the hybrids can have flowers the size of dinner plates (up to 10 inches [25cm] across), I prefer the wild species with its saucer-size flowers in pink or white since it doesn't seem such a freak of nature.

'Southern Belle' and 'Disco Belle' are very similar, offering a wide color range that includes white, pink, red, and crimson—all with contrasting eyes. Yet the first-year growth of 'Southern Belle' can top 6 feet (1.8m), while 'Disco Belle' remains more compact at 3 to 4 feet (90 to 120cm). Both are easily propagated by seed, sown 8 to 10 weeks before the last expected frost in spring. Soak the seeds overnight or chip the bullet-hard skin with a razor blade to speed germination. The wild species is more easily propagated by division. Although plants are killed by frost, they will overwinter even in frozen soil to bloom year after year. Give them full sun and a deep, fertile, humus-rich, moist soil.

Since the flowers of the hardy hybrid hibiscus 'Southern Belle' can measure up to 10 inches (25cm) across, they are ideal for decorating the edges of large ponds.

Hosta sieboldiana 'Elegans'

(blue hosta)

'Elegans' hosta grows huge, heart-shaped, dusky blue leaves that are richly textured with prominent leaf veins and a crinkled surface. The leaves can grow to 2 feet (60cm) long and the plants spread to 4 feet (1.2m) wide, though in a fertile, humus-rich, moist soil they can grow even bigger. In early summer, plants produce erect flower stems clustered with trumpet-shaped, pale lavender flowers tapered to a spike. One of the finest bog plants for water gardens, blue hosta looks striking with blue flag irises, Japanese primroses, ostrich ferns, and false spiraea.

The whole family of hostas offers many beautiful foliage effects. If you have the space, it's good to put together a collection of contrasting kinds. 'Sum and Substance' has shiny, chartreuse leaves that are even larger than 'Elegans', while 'So Sweet' is a lively green-and-white variegated form with the bonus of fragrant flowers. In full sun hosta leaves can become scorched. They perform best in a lightly shaded location. Propagation is by division after flowering.

An assortment of hostas—with 'Elegans' planted in the center—cover a slope bordering a pond. Flowers can be blue, purple, or white, depending on the variety, and some are delightfully fragrant.

Houttuynia cordata

(chameleon plant)

An interesting bonus of this beautiful creeping hardy perennial is its edible leaves, which can be cooked and used as a spinach substitute. With a flavor like bitter oranges, however, it is an acquired taste, and its ornamental value is reason enough to grow it. Small, ivylike leaves display three colors—red, green, and yellow—with the best color performance in a sunny location. In summer the vines are also covered with small, star-shaped white flowers. I like to partner it with another spreading aquatic edible, watercress, for the strong contrast of its dark green leaves.

Plants grow to 9 inches (22.5cm) high and spread several feet wide in a season. Though the tops die down in winter, the roots will survive to come back each year. We grow chameleon plant in moist, humus-rich soil and use it like a fleece to drape over rock ledges and cascade into the water. We also have it in pots submerged 6 inches (15cm) below the surface to soften the edges of our informal pools. I have seen this colorful foliage plant cultivated in submerged pots to completely encircle a formal pool. Propagate by division of the stoloniferous roots.

Above: A chameleon plant will grow with its roots submerged in water or in pockets of moist soil among rocks bordering a pool. Below: This close-up of a water poppy flower is approximately life size.

Hydrocleys nymphoides

(*water poppy*)

The flowers of this tender tropical aquatic plant look like yellow California poppies! Blooming all summer, it prefers full sun but will tolerate light shade. The floating foliage is glossy, green, and oval, making a dense weave across the surface of water. Though a floating plant, its roots need to be anchored in soil. It looks attractive partnered with tropical waterlilies and water lettuce.

Confine the roots to a pot submerged in 6 to 12 inches (15 to 30cm) of water. In winter, move the pot indoors to a heated holding tank, since water poppy is injured by frost. The leaves are evergreen, and the plants are easily propagated by division.

Ilex verticillata

(*winterberry*)

This deciduous holly is native to the northeastern United States, where it grows in swamps, often with its roots covered with shallow water. Inconspicuous white flowers in spring are followed by masses of red berries in autumn, bringing color to ponds and stream banks at a time when the landscape begins to look bleak. Berries are formed only on female plants, following cross-pollination from a male, but one male can pollinate a grove of females. Often, cross-pollination occurs from male American hollies.

At Cedaridge Farm we create a spectacular winter color display by partnering winterberry with switch grass. Winterberry's red berries harmonize with the dried orange leaf blades of switch grass, which persists all winter. Some very fine hybrid varieties have been developed, notably 'Winter King' and 'Sparkleberry'. There are also orange-berried forms. Plants prefer full sun and a humus-rich, moist soil, and spread by forming a thicket of stoloniferous roots. Propagation is from tip cuttings taken in spring.

Winterberry shows its upright habit and berry-laden branches against the wintry reflections of a small pond. The berries are relished by bluebirds.

Iris ensata

(*Japanese iris*)

Also known as *I. kaempferi*, the Japanese iris is invaluable as a summer-flowering marginal plant with roots submerged in shallow water, though it also thrives in boggy soil. In addition to large, flat flower heads in white and shades of blue and purple, the sword-shaped leaves are ornamental all year. The 'Higo' strain is a particularly fine selection with large flowers, many measuring 8 inches (20cm) across. My favorites among the 'Higo' varieties are 'Capricorn Butterfly', a pale blue with purple leaf veins, and 'Thunder & Lightning', a deep royal purple with flashes of yellow at the base of each petal.

Perfect companions for Japanese iris, which is the last of the iris family to bloom, are maiden grass, ostrich ferns, waterlilies, and false spiraea. It can be planted in drifts of separate colors or as a mixture. Give Japanese irises full sun and a fertile, humus-rich, acid soil. Plants grow to 4 feet (1.2m) high and form vigorous clumps from spreading rhizomes. Plants are hardy and propagate easily from division.

Japanese irises will quickly colonize moist soil, growing even where their roots are covered with shallow water.

Iris, Louisiana hybrids

(*Louisiana iris*)

Similar in appearance to yellow and blue flag irises, Louisiana iris is a catchall name for species of iris found in southern swamps and their hybrids. The species include *I. fulva* (a brick red immortalized by the bird artist Audubon in his painting of the Parula warbler), *I. giganticaerulea* (the tallest blue, reaching 5 feet [1.5m]), *I. brevicaulis* (a dwarf growing only 2 feet [60cm] high), *I. hexagona*, and *I. nelsonii* (of medium height at 3 to 4 feet [90 to 120cm]). They are hardy even into Canada, and their special claim to fame is a wide color range including red, orange, yellow, purple, white, and many shades of blue. Flower form can vary from flat flower heads resembling Japanese irises to upright flower forms resembling flag irises. Since they spread quickly from rhizomes, they are at their best massed along stream banks and around ponds. They thrive in boggy, humus-rich soil and soil covered with shallow water.

Plants grow 2 to 5 feet (60 to 150cm) high, depending on species and cultivar. More than five hundred cultivars are available, but the most popular tend to be 'Professor Neil', a rich red, and 'Delta Star', a dark blue streaked with yellow that looks like an upward-facing clematis. They need at least 6 hours of sun a day to flower well. Propagate by dividing the rhizome mass in late summer or early autumn. Cover the rhizomes with at least 1 inch (2.5cm) of soil.

The iris 'Dorothea K. Williamson', like other irises in the Louisiana group, is hardy in northern gardens, though this collection of species originated in the southernmost areas of the United States.

Iris pseudacorus
(yellow flag iris)

At Cedaridge Farm one of the most beautiful sights for visitors is a planting in our marsh garden that combines the golden flowers of yellow flag iris with the sapphire blue flowers of blue flag iris (*I. versicolor*) and an underplanting of blue forget-me-nots. They bloom together in a color harmony that Monet made famous in a painting of irises, which a visitor to his garden described as "the gold and sapphire of an artist's dreams." Another stunning color combination is to contrast yellow flag iris with red Japanese primroses or orange candelabra primroses. Plants have slender, pointed, sword-shaped leaves that can grow to 4 feet (1.2m) high with loads of yellow flowers that bloom in spring. There is a variegated form, 'Variegata', with creamy yellow leaves that make an effective vertical accent at the margin of pools and ponds, though it tends to be sparse-flowering.

Yellow flag iris prefers a clay soil to support its erect habit. It also likes full sun but tolerates light shade better than most other marsh irises. Propagate by dividing the rhizomes at any time and covering them with at least 1 inch (2.5cm) of soil in a bog or shallow water. Yellow flag iris also self-seeds readily. Native to Europe, it has naturalized throughout North America.

In an area at Cedaridge Farm we call the stream garden, a prolific colony of yellow flag irises grows beside a bridge.

Iris versicolor

(*blue flag iris*)

Native to the northeastern United States, this looks similar to the Japanese flag iris (*I. laevigata)*. It blooms in spring with sapphire blue flowers and looks sensational partnered with yellow flag iris. Plants grow to 3 feet (90cm) high and spread by rhizomes. They will grow in shallow water but do best in a boggy, humus-rich soil. Propagate by division of the rhizome colonies after flowering.

In the world of irises there are many other good species and cultivars suitable for boggy conditions, but special mention should be made of Siberian iris (*I. sibirica)*, which resembles the blue flag iris in flower form. It is available in dozens of cultivars, some dwarf (2 feet [60cm] tall) and some standard (up to 4 feet [1.2m]). Though not long in flower, they are extremely free-flowering in shades of blue and yellow, plus white, especially in sun. In autumn the leaves have the bonus of collapsing in a fountainlike clump and turning golden. They grow dense clusters of fleshy roots that are easily divided.

Siberian irises are mostly shades of blue, but white and yellow also exist. They bloom at the same time as yellow flag irises.

Juncus effusus

(*c o r k s c r e w   r u s h*)

There are more than three hundred species and cultivars of rush suitable for pools and ponds. Many are evergreen, and most have dark green needlelike leaves that grow in a spiky clump from 1 to 6 feet (30 to 180cm) high, depending on the variety. The unique cultivar 'Spiralis' is distinct in that the semievergreen leaves curl in a spiral, creating an interesting foliage effect that can enhance plantings that rely on foliage contrasts. The flowers occur as small brown clusters at the top of the leaves. Plants are particularly beautiful when used in company with other bog-loving grasses such as 'Bowles Golden' grass and snowy woodrush (*Luzula nivea*), which produces clouds of soft creamy flower clusters in spring.

Both corkscrew rush and snowy woodrush are best used as marginal plants, confined to pots, with their rims positioned just below the waterline. Use them singly or in groups of three for good effect. Best propagated by division in spring, the plants grow in sun or shade, with light shade preferable in areas with hot, dry summers.

Corkscrew rush is planted in a submerged container in front of a clump of maiden grass in one of the pools at Wave Hill Garden, New York.

Lemna minor
(*duckweed*)

Avaluable fish and waterfowl food, this hardy floating plant can be a beautiful embellishment to informal water gardens, but if not controlled it can completely cover the surface, making the water look choked with algae. To keep it within bounds, use a long-handled net to scoop up excessive growth; you'll need a pair of waders for cleaning large ponds. Scoop up the weed, dump it in the sun to dry, and then remove it to a compost pile. When you buy plants in pots from aquatic centers, invariably duckweed will hitch a ride on the soil or around the rim of the pots. Thus you don't need to purchase it, though aquatic centers will gladly sell you some in a plastic bag filled with water.

Plants do not need to be rooted in soil and do well in sun or light shade. The small, round leaves spread in all directions. At the onset of freezing weather, the foliage sinks to the bottom of the pond to overwinter in a dormant condition. Then, at the onset of warm weather, the fragments of foliage rise to the surface to begin new growth. Flowers are tiny, green, and inconspicuous. Propagate at any time by dividing an existing colony and keeping it wet until it can be floated in a new location.

When duckweed covers a pool completely, as seen here, it should be scooped up with a net. Otherwise the lack of light may harm fish.

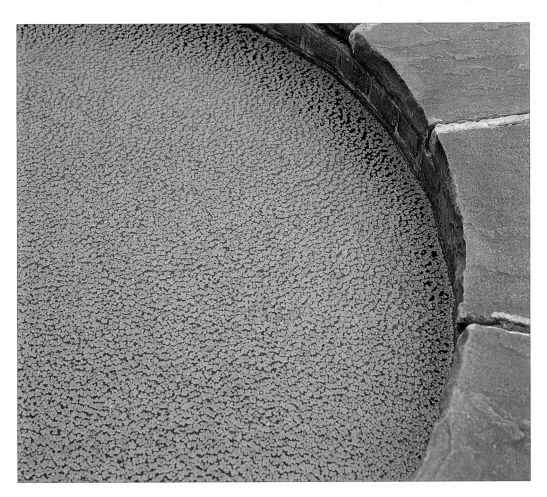

Ligularia dentata 'Desdemona'

(bronze-leaf ragwort)

There are several beautiful ligularias suitable for boggy, humus-rich soils in sun or light shade. *L. stenocephala* 'The Rocket' has dark green, triangular, toothed leaves and tapering yellow flower heads. *L. dentata* 'Desdemona' and 'Othello' are very similar, displaying circular, shiny bronze leaves that are bright purple on the underside. All have a commanding presence in the landscape, especially planted as bold colonies, though 'Othello' and 'Desdemona' both have an architectural or sculptural quality that allows them to be planted alone.

Flowers are yellow, shaped like daisies, and produced in large flat clusters that can measure several feet across. Flowering height is 5 to 6 feet (1.5 to 1.8m). Unfortunately, all these ligularias have an annoying habit of wilting during the heat of the day, especially in full sun. To avoid wilting, grow in light shade and boggy soil mulched to keep the roots cool. Good companions are false spiraea, ostrich ferns, Japanese irises, and blue hostas. Propagation is by division.

A beautiful pondside planting spotlights bronze-leaf ragwort in full flower. Ragwort makes a good flowering companion for summer-blooming false spiraea.

Lobelia cardinalis

(cardinal flower)

At Cedaridge Farm we found wild colonies of cardinal flowers growing along our stream bank. To increase them, we dug up those with a cluster of leaf rosettes, then divided them. We also transplanted dozens of small seedlings that we found further downstream growing in shallow water. In summer we admire their dark red flowers, which contrast well with the silvery leaves of variegated maiden grass. Plants grow to 4 feet (1.2m) high with dark spear-shaped leaves. Every morning and late afternoon we can guarantee the appearance of hummingbirds, which are attracted by the color and drops of nectar in each tubular floret.

Plants prefer a humus-rich, boggy soil in sun or light shade. There are several species of lobelia, with *L. cardinalis* the hardiest. Also hardy is the blue-flowered species, *L. siphilitica*, blooming at the same time as the red. A Mexican species, *L. fulgens*, has large crimson flower spikes and bronze foliage. It is commonly seen in Pacific Coast gardens, but it is not hardy in areas where the ground freezes. Though division is the easiest form of propagation, plants take only one season to reach flowering size from seed. Started in spring or summer, flowers will bloom the following year.

Above: Cardinal flowers grow in company with cattails. Both will thrive with their roots covered in shallow water. Below: Mosaic plant floats on the surface of water, its fascinating foliage creating a good contrast to smooth waterlily leaves.

Ludwigia peploides
(mosaic plant)

An unusual floating plant native to ponds and lakes from the Pacific Northwest to South America, mosaic plant has distinctive diamond-shaped leaves that splay out like a starburst. The leaves cluster together in such precise patterns that on close examination they appear to be a tile mosaic, hence its common name. In addition to its beautiful leaves, the plant produces cheerful yellow cup-shaped blooms in early summer.

Mosaic plant prefers full sun; it is a moderately tender perennial killed by freezing temperatures. Its roots should be anchored in a pot of soil, and at the onset of frost the pot should be moved indoors to a frost-free holding tank. Alternatively, visit an aquatic center each year and purchase new potted plants for the season. Propagate by seeds, division of roots, and cuttings.

Handsome flower spathes of yellow skunk cabbage appear in early spring. This plant is unfairly named, however, since it does not have the objectionable odor of its cousin, eastern skunk cabbage.

Lysichiton americanum
(y e l l o w   s k u n k   c a b b a g e)

Native to marshes of the Pacific Northwest, this is one of the earliest water plants to bloom in spring. What a sight it is as it strikes through moist soil to display clusters of pointed yellow hoods followed by translucent, spear-shaped, wavy green leaves that can grow to 5 feet (1.5m) high. The common name is a misnomer, for the plant has a slightly sweet fragrance, though it's related to the less desirable brown-flowered skunk cabbage of the Northeast.

Popular in British water gardens, yellow skunk cabbage is hardy into New England but rarely seen in the Northeast. It certainly deserves to be much more widely grown, especially with other early flowering bog plants such as marsh marigolds and forget-me-nots. Plants can survive with their roots permanently submerged in shallow water. Yellow skunk cabbage grows best in light shade, and is beautiful planted in colonies along stream margins. Propagation is by division.

Lysimachia nummularia
(c r e e p i n g   J e n n y)

Many species of *Lysimachia* make beautiful flowering bog plants, including *L. punctata* with its yellow flower spikes and *L. clethroides* with its white flower spikes shaped like goose necks. Both form colonies of upright plants 3 to 4 feet (90 to 120cm) high. Creeping Jenny, however, is a marvelous spreading perennial that creates a tight knit of round leaves, creeping over boulders and boggy ground and floating freely on the surface of water. It has the added bonus of cheerful yellow buttercuplike flowers that present a carpet of gold in summer. The cultivar 'Aurea' has bright golden leaves.

Plants grow no more than 1 inch (2.5cm) high and spread to several feet wide. Give them a boggy, humus-rich soil close to flat boulders and still water so that they can create a fleecelike effect. Site them in sun or light shade. Propagation is by division. Though plants are native to Europe, creeping Jenny has naturalized throughout North America from self-seeding.

Above: Creeping Jenny scrambles over boulders and will dip its yellow flowering stems into and across water. Below: Elegant ostrich ferns have a commanding presence in the landscape.

Matteuccia struthiopteris
(*ostrich fern*)

Called German ferns in Europe, these handsome hardy perennials are native to the damp woodlands of the northeastern United States. They are undoubtedly the best of many fern varieties for stream and pond margins. The erect fronds stand 4 feet (1.2m) high and are arranged in a crown to form a shape like a shuttlecock. They are particularly striking when backlit by a rising or setting sun. Use them singly or in groups, especially in company with hostas and Japanese primroses. The young, unfolding fronds—known as fiddleheads—are a delicacy when boiled or sautéed like asparagus tips.

Plants prefer a humus-rich, permanently moist soil and will survive long periods with their roots submerged in shallow water. In boggy soil, ostrich ferns reproduce from stoloniferous roots and form colonies. These can be dug up, the underground "umbilical cord" being cut for propagation. Also, individual root crowns are made up of bulblets shaped like a knuckle, each capable of forming a new plant when detached in spring, before the fronds unfurl.

Metasequoia glyptostroboides

(dawn redwood)

Until the 1940s, when a botanical expedition from the Arnold Arboretum in Boston found a small grove of these hardy coniferous trees growing along the Yangtze River in China, this beautiful spirelike conifer was believed to have been extinct in the wild for millions of years. Since its introduction into North American gardens it has proven to be one of the best trees for boggy soils, growing up to 5 feet (1.5m) a year in a pyramidal shape. The soft, needlelike leaves resemble hemlock foliage. Though they are similar in appearance to evergreens, the leaves are in fact deciduous, changing to a golden color in late autumn. The trunks have reddish brown, shedding bark, flared at the base like swamp cypress and fluted to present a prehistoric appearance.

Plants grow to 80 feet (24m) tall and must be planted at least 10 feet (3m) apart. At Cedaridge Farm we have a grove of eleven trees growing along our stream, but dawn redwood would also look attractive planted singly. Plants are propagated from seed and softwood cuttings. Rooting occurs within 4 months, but the lead shoot may be damaged in severe weather. A new leader, however, will form quickly to continue its rapid growth.

Another desirable waterside tree is the bald or swamp cypress. Though not reliably hardy north of New York City, it has the added distinction of being able to grow with its roots permanently submerged in water and of producing knobbly cypress "knees" that protrude around the trunk.

This forty-year-old grove of dawn redwood shades the stream bank through three seasons. Though they lose their leaves in winter they maintain an attractive appearance.

Miscanthus sinensis

(*m a i d e n   g r a s s*)

Dozens of varieties of maiden grass exist. Leaf blades may be slender or broad, and autumn foliage amber or red. Some cultivars grow silky white flower plumes in late summer, while others bear red flower plumes in autumn. A variegated form is desirable as a waterside planting because its white-striped leaf blades present a distinctive silvery appearance when viewed from a distance. This silver coloration is extremely beautiful as a background to red, pink, and orange flowers. At Cedaridge Farm we also admire the variety 'Zebrinus' for its unusual golden yellow variegation. Instead of running longitudinally, the variegation is horizontal, giving the appearance of a shower of sparks. All prefer a sunny location.

Variegated maiden grass thrives in moist soil, and looks especially beautiful when planted beside weeping willows and evergreen shrubs.

Most maiden grasses grow to 6 feet (1.8m) high with an equal spread and form a fountainlike cascade of slender leaves that turn amber in autumn. 'Variegatus' has silky red flower plumes that appear in late summer. They persist well into winter and make good dried arrangements.

Myosotis scorpioides

(*w a t e r   f o r g e t - m e - n o t*)

Also known as *M. palustris*, this low, spreading, hardy perennial is indistinguishable in outward appearance from the common garden forget-me-not. It grows small, spear-shaped leaves and clouds of blue flowers in such profusion that a mass planting looks like a blue mist hovering over water. The water forget-me-not thrives in boggy soil and will even spread into shallow water. We like to plant this charming flower along a sparkling stream. During floods it sometimes gets washed away, but it always seems to come back from torn roots and self-seeding.

Plants grow to 18 inches (45cm) high, spread 2¹/₂ feet (75cm), and prefer a humus-rich, boggy soil in sun or light shade. They are perfect partners to hostas, yellow and blue flag irises, and Japanese and candelabra primroses. Propagation is by seed and by division.

Left: Once you have planted water forget-me-nots along a stream they are likely to come back every year because they self-seed. Below: Parrot's feather contrasts pleasingly with waterlily foliage.

Myriophyllum aquaticum

(*parrot's feather*)

Most reference books say parrot's feather is a tender tropical plant that is killed by frost. True, its attractive, feathery foliage does brown after frost, but at Cedaridge Farm it overwinters from dormant roots that remain in the soil, and that means it's hardy! Though classified as a submerged oxygenating plant, much of its growth is on the water surface. In southern gardens it has the potential to spread as rapidly as duckweed and completely cover a large pond in a single season. If this type of growth does threaten to overtake your pond, take a net, put on some waders, and scoop it up. Leave it in the sun to dry for a few hours and then remove it to a compost pile.

Plants never grow more than 4 to 6 inches (10 to 15cm) high but will spread several inches a day during warm, sunny weather. Although tolerant of light shade, parrot's feather prefers full sun and humus-rich soil with the roots covered by shallow water. Confine the roots to a container and sink the container below the ice level to overwinter, or remove it indoors to a holding tank. Use it in combination with other floating and submerged plants, especially near waterlily foliage, duckweed, water poppy, and mosaic plant. Propagate by division, using any stem section with roots.

Nasturtium officinale

(*w a t e r c r e s s*)

If you have a slow-moving stream or a shallow pond or pool, it would be a sad omission not to grow any watercress, since it is an attractive plant with small oval leaflets arranged like a fan and small star-shaped white flowers that appear in summer. The leaves are delicious raw as a nutritious piquant salad green, cooked like spinach, or chopped fine and blended with onion to make a hearty soup. There is hardly a day of the year when the leaves cannot be harvested. In cool months the plants remain on the surface of the water as compact, floating rosettes. In summer, the stems may elongate and stand up to 12 inches (30cm) above the water's surface.

Watercress is a hardy, edible plant that likes to be rooted in shallow water, where it spreads by runners. In streams that do not freeze leaves can be harvested virtually year-round.

To introduce watercress into your water garden, purchase plants from aquatic plant specialists or grow it from seed purchased from mail-order sources. Simply choose a sunny location and push the roots into sandy, gravelly, or clay soil, and anchor in place with a stone.

Nelumbo nucifera

(*s a c r e d   l o t u s*)

Deceptively tender in appearance because of its tropical origins, lotuses are remarkably hardy and will generally overwinter in clay soils that remain below the ice line. American lotus (*N. lutea*) is a small, yellow-flowered species native to southern lakes. The most popular varieties for water gardens, however, are the pink or white sacred lotus, made famous by Japanese and Egyptian artisans as symbols of beauty and fertility. The fragrant lotus flower starts as a large oval bud up to 18 inches (45cm) high. It unfolds to take the shape of a waterlily atop tall, slender stems. The bud opens early in the morning and closes by mid-afternoon. After the third day the petals drop. A cone-shaped seedpod develops, turning brown when ripe. Through holes in the seed cone, you can see hard,

Lotus blossoms are large and usually pink or white. Flowers are followed by wide flat seedheads that rattle when shaken. When fully dried, the seedheads make a good addition to a dried flower arrangement.

round, pea-size seeds that rattle when the pod is shaken. These dried seedpods are valued by flower arrangers. Plants bloom for 6 to 8 weeks in midsummer. The parasol-shaped leaves are ornamental even when the plants are not in bloom.

Plants grow to 7 feet (2.1m) tall, require 5 to 6 hours of sunlight a day, and need their roots covered by 2 to 4 inches (5 to 10cm) of soil below 6 to 12 inches (15 to 30cm) of water. Flowering does not begin until several weeks of 80°F (27°C) temperatures have warmed the water, which makes lotuses difficult to grow in some parts of the Pacific Northwest, Canada, and Alaska. Propagate by division of fleshy tubers. They may not bloom until the second year after division. If you have room for only one cultivar, make it 'Mrs. Perry D. Slocum', which changes color from creamy yellow to soft pink.

Nymphaea hybrids

(*w a t e r l i l i e s*)

Waterlilies are the most important plant family for pools and ponds, with floating islands of round leaves and large flowers in the shape of a starburst. They are classified as hardy (surviving severe winters below the ice line) and tender (requiring protection of a heated indoor holding tank during cold winters). Most varieties sold are hybrids of wild species. The hardy species are found growing in Europe, North America, and Mexico, while the tropical come mostly from Africa and Australia. Both kinds like their roots to be covered with 6 to 12 inches (15 to 30cm) of water. If a leaf is allowed to dry, it dies.

The color range of the hardies includes red, yellow, orange, pink, and white (some of which are delightfully fragrant). Color range of the tropicals is similar but also includes blue. The flowers of hardies float on the surface of the water, while tropicals stand aloft on slender stems up to 9 inches (22.5cm) long.

Tropicals are larger-flowered, bloom for up to 2 months longer than the hardies, and can be day-blooming or night-blooming. Many varieties are fragrant. Most require 5 to 6 hours of sunlight. To bloom strongly, they need regular feeding with special high-phosphorus fertilizer tablets pushed into the soil around the roots.

Claude Monet made famous the first hardy waterlily hybrids, which were developed by Joseph Bory Latour-Marliac. Many of the beautiful hybrids Monet grew, such as 'Chromatella' (yellow) and 'Escarboucle' (rosy red), are still popular today. He was not able to grow tropicals outdoors because his pond water was too cool in summer, but over most parts of North America hot summers provide ideal conditions. Overwinter tropicals in a heated holding tank and do not move outdoors until the water temperature is at least 70°F (21°C). A beautiful tropical variety is 'Albert Greenberg' for its extra-large rosy pink flowers with yellow highlights and its marbled foliage.

Propagate waterlilies by division in spring. The hardies have rhizomes that should be cut into 5-inch (12.5cm) sections so that each section has a set of roots and a crown of leaves. They should be planted at a 45-degree angle, crown side up. Tropicals are divided by separating the root mass into small self-contained clumps. Position them perpendicularly so that the roots are down and the crown of leaves points upward.

The tropical waterlily 'Albert Greenberg' is noted for its decorative floating marbled leaves and large glowing pink flowers held above the water.

Nymphoides indica

(*water snowflake*)

This floating tender perennial merely needs its roots anchored in a pot of soil to create an island of rounded, heart-shaped, mottled green-and-brown leaves and masses of star-shaped yellow flowers with fringed petals that resemble snowflakes. There is a white-flowered form, *N. cristata*, with plain green leaves. Grow them side by side, allowing the pots to sit so that the rims are 3 to 12 inches (7.5 to 30cm) below the waterline. Move them indoors to a heated holding tank wherever there are repeated frosts in winter.

Plants hug the water, but the flowers are held up about 3 inches (7.5cm) on slender stalks. Give them full sun and humus-rich soil, and they will bloom for several months in summer. They are good companions to water poppies, mosaic plant, and parrot's feather. Propagation is by division.

Left: The delicate fringed flowers of water snowflake are appropriately named. Below: Flowers of the umbrella plant bloom in early spring on naked stems, before the large leaves appear.

Peltiphyllum peltatum
(umbrella plant)

When you have a pond or stream with plenty of space to fill in the background, search out some bog-loving plants with giant leaves, for they can create an ethereal quality. Umbrella plant is a hardy perennial, valued for serrated, parasol-shaped leaves and curious naked flower stalks topped by pale pink, flat flower clusters that appear in early spring before the leaves emerge. Native to high alpine streams in California's Sierra Nevada mountains, umbrella plant has rhizomes that knit together in boggy soil to create a dense root mass that controls soil erosion.

Plants grow to 10 feet (3m) tall with each leaf as much as 2 feet (60cm) across. Use them in combination with blue hostas, Chilean rhubarb, and Japanese coltsfoot. They grow in sun or shade and prefer a humus-rich, loam soil. Propagate by division.

Petasites japonicus 'Gigantea'
(giant Japanese coltsfoot)

I recently read an article by a neophyte water gardener who declared that his biggest mistake was planting this hardy perennial around his pond, since it spread into unwanted areas and even pushed its roots under walls to invade other parts of the garden. Certainly, the giant Japanese coltsfoot needs space to spread, preferably at a pond's edge. At Cedaridge Farm, however, we grow it under groups of 'Heritage' river birch, creating one of the most admired plant partnerships on the property. In Monet's garden at Giverny, giant Japanese coltsfoot is grown with yellow groove bamboo and weeping willows. Their foliage contrast is striking.

Giant Japanese coltsfoot grow among 'Heritage' river birch in a dramatic pond-side planting. Coltsfoot needs plenty of room, and it should be confined to an area where it will not become invasive.

Plants grow to 5 feet (1.5m) tall and produce velvety, heart-shaped leaves that can measure 3 feet (90cm) across. Plant in sun or light shade. Coltsfoot has aggressive stoloniferous roots that send up unusual, cone-shaped, lime green flower clusters in early spring before the leaves appear. On hot days the leaves may wilt. Propagate by division.

Pistia stratiotes
(water lettuce)

These floating tender perennials produce rosettes of decorative silver-green leaves that resemble a small, tightly bunched lettuce. In frost-free climates like southern Florida they can spread at a prodigious rate, quickly covering a small pond and crowding out everything except water hyacinths. In northern gardens, however, they are not so aggressive and are killed by frost unless overwintered in a heated holding tank.

Plants grow to 4 inches (10cm) high, spread out in all directions to create floating islands, and do not need their roots anchored in soil. Water lettuce prefers full sun. It is generally used with water hyacinths and water poppies to create a tapestry of foliage on the water surface. Propagate by division.

Left: In frost-free climates water lettuce can completely cover a large pond with its floating rosettes in a single season. Below: Hardy snakeweed is an eye-catching flowering plant for pondsides.

Polygonum bistorta 'Superbum'
(*snakeweed*)

From the damp meadows of north-ern Europe to the Arctic circle, this easy-to-grow pondside plant is also known as *Persicaria* as a result of a change in botanical nomenclature. Many species of *Polygonum* are suitable for boggy soils, but 'Superbum' is the showiest, producing light pink, pokerlike flowers in great profusion during late spring and early summer. A hardy perennial, it forms a dense mat of spear-shaped, semievergreen leaves, with flowers 3 inches (7.5cm) long on slender stems that can reach 3 feet (90cm) high. Use them to line footpaths beside ponds or streams and as naturalized colonies growing at the water's edge.

'Superbum' looks especially beautiful with forget-me-nots, ferns, hostas, yellow flag irises, and Japanese primroses. Plants prefer full sun but tolerate light shade. They like a humus-rich, moist soil and excel as a display flower when planted next to rock walls or boulders. Propagation is by division after flowering.

Pontederia cordata

(pickerel weed)

The beautiful arrow-shaped leaves and blue flowers of pickerel weed appear in summer. In small pools the roots should be confined to a submerged pot.

There are both white- and blue-flowering varieties of this clump-forming hardy perennial, which grows arrow-straight stems topped with spikelike flower clusters. Plants grow to 4 feet (1.2m) high and display attractive, olive green, arrow-shaped leaves. They thrive either in boggy soil or with their roots covered with up to 12 inches (30cm) of water. Flowers start to appear in late spring and continue nonstop until autumn frosts.

Native to tidal marshes of the mid-Atlantic and New England, plants can become invasive if left to their own devices, so it is best to confine their roots to pots. Grow pickerel weed with graceful cattails, arrowhead, and thalia. Flowering is inhibited by shade, but the decorative leaves still make a beautiful display. Plants tolerate a wide range of soils, including clay and sandy soil. Propagate by division in spring.

Primula species and hybrids

(*bog primroses*)

Japanese and candelabra primroses both like boggy soil and will self-seed to form large colonies. These 'Inshriach' hybrids were developed in Scotland.

There are many beautiful species of primroses, mostly native to China and Japan, that thrive in boggy soils. Collectively known as bog primroses or candelabra primroses, these include *P. japonica* (Japanese primroses, in shades of red and pink), *P. helodoxa* (bright yellow), and *P. florindae* (the giant yellow Himalayan cowslip). My favorite color mixture is *P. × hybrida* 'Imshriach'. One of many hybrid candelabra primroses, it is similar to *P. × beesiana* in its color range of red, orange, purple, and yellow, but is even richer.

The Japanese primrose is the easiest to grow, provided it has a constantly moist soil. It likes to grow along slow-moving streams and in boggy soil beside ponds, especially when there is plenty of humus content. Plants grow to 3 feet (90cm) high and flower in spring. The leaves are oval and heavily crinkled, forming a rosette. Slender flower stems grow from the center of each rosette, with the flowers arranged in whorls at the top. They are sensational planted in sun or light shade among clumps of hostas and ostrich ferns. Propagation is by seed and by division. Once a colony of several plants is established, they self-seed rapidly to become self-perpetuating.

Rodgersia aesculifolia

(horsechestnut plant)

Several look-alike species are hard to tell apart by the foliage. Only when they bloom can you see a significant difference. *R. aesculifolia's* large lustrous leaves, composed of serrated leaflets spread out like a fan, resemble those of a buckeye tree. The flowers are held high above the foliage on slender stems, forming a cloud of pale pink flowers. A similar species, *R. pinnata*, has less attractive foliage but has a cultivar, 'Superba', that produces beautiful, deep pink flower clusters and bronze leaves.

Plants grow 3 to 4 feet (90 to 120cm) high and spread by underground rhizomes to form a colony. Unless grown in light shade and boggy soil, the leaves scorch easily, turning brown at the edges. Use horsechestnut plant with other large-leaf waterside plants, especially hostas, umbrella plants, and Japanese coltsfoot. Horsechestnut plant prefers a boggy, humus-rich soil. Propagation is by division of established clumps.

Horsechestnut plant has decorative textured leaves and the bonus of frothy white or pink flower clusters in late spring. Here they make a good counterpoint to spirelike foxgloves.

Sagittaria latifolia

(arrowhead)

Several species of arrowhead are suitable for growing in ponds, especially when their roots are covered with up to 12 inches (30cm) of water. *S. latifolia* is the best of the hardy perennial species, while *S. montevidensis* is larger-flowered but tender. All are identified by leaves shaped like an arrowhead, held above the water on long stems up to 3 feet (90cm) high. The flowers are three-petaled, white, and borne in summer in clusters among the leaves.

Plant in full sun and confine to pots, using a humus-rich, clay soil. They are particularly attractive in the company of cattails, papyrus, umbrella palm, and irises, where the display of different foliage shapes can present a tapestry of greens. Propagate by division.

Left: Arrowhead can be confined to submerged pots to create good structural accents in small ponds. Below: Pitcher plants are hardy as long as the soil remains moist and is not subjected to a hard freeze.

Sarracenia leucophylla
(pitcher plant)

Many species of pitcher plant are native from the New Jersey Pine Barrens to the Gulf states. Though tender to hard freezes, they are proving to be hardier than was previously supposed, especially when sited in a special boggy soil of almost pure peat in a sheltered location. They are insectivorous plants (sometimes erroneously called carnivorous), trapping their prey by extending up from their roots a tubular fusion of leaves with a flat hooded roof over an opening. Insects drawn to the opening by scent crawl down and fall into a puddle of digestive juices that dissolve the insect and absorb it as a source of food. The most prized species is *S. leucophylla* because of its distinctive white pitchers heavily veined in red. When backlit by a rising or setting sun, the pitchers glow like Chinese lanterns. The plants also produce curious nodding purple flowers in spring.

Plants grow to 4 feet (1.2m) high from a clump of slender leaves and produce rhizomatous roots that can be divided. They are best planted to form a colony in company with other insectivorous plants, notably sundews, Venus flytraps, and cobra lilies (though some of these are tender and may need overwintering in a holding tank). At the Atlanta Botanical Garden there is a magnificent collection of pitcher plants, many of them grown outdoors year-round in containers.

Thalia dealbata

(w a t e r   c a n n a)

At first glance, this hardy perennial for water margins looks like a tender banana plant with broad, spear-shaped leaves. In summer, however, it sends up tall, slender flower stems topped with clusters of lavender-blue flowers held high above the foliage. The leaves generally stand 3 to 4 feet (90 to 120cm) above the water, and the flowers may add an additional 3 feet (90cm). There is a taller species, the red-stemmed thalia (*T. geniculata* 'Ruminoides'), with red stems and flower spikes that can grow to 10 feet (3m) high.

Plants are best confined to large pots and covered with up to 12 inches (30cm) of water. They look sensational in formal pools and are a good complement to other large water plants such as tropical waterlilies, lotuses, and the giant Amazon waterlily. Give them a sunny position and clay soil. Propagation is by division.

Water cannas are a favorite embellishment for formal pools. This one, together with giant Amazon waterlilies, provides a good view from the nearby bench.

Typha latifolia

(c a t t a i l)

This is the common broad-leaf cattail found naturalized across great stretches of marshy meadows, tidal ponds, and stream banks of North America. In spring it produces cigar-shaped brown blooms that, by summer's end, turn into fluffy white seed bodies that float off into the wind to seed themselves in boggy soils. Since plants can be invasive with their aggressive, stoloniferous roots, it is best to confine them to a pot submerged in up to 12 inches (30cm) of water. Several other species are suitable for water gardens. *T. angustifolia*, the narrow-leaf cattail, has a more graceful appearance because of its slender leaves, whereas *T. minima* is a dwarf form that grows to just 2 feet (60cm) high.

Cattails prefer full sun and are not fussy about soil, growing well in both clay and sand. The tall kinds look spectacular in wildlife ponds, and draw ducks and other waterfowl to nest among them. The long, flowering stems are valued by flower arrangers for dried arrangements. They are best propagated by division after flowering.

Above: Cattails produce dense, dark brown seedheads in spring and early summer. Left: The tender Amazon waterlily has a white flower that smells like a pineapple and changes to pink as it ages.

Victoria amazonica

(giant Amazon waterlily)

The leaves of this tender, tropical, floating plant can exceed 10 feet (3m) in width and support the weight of a child. The large waterlily–like flowers open white with a fragrance like a pineapple and turn pink with age. Discovered along streams running through the Amazon rain forest, the plants are tender to frost. When grown in a large tub, however, the roots can be overwintered in a heated holding tank after the leaves have died back. The tub can move outdoors when the water temperature exceeds 70°F (21°C). Above this temperature, the giant Amazon waterlily grows exceedingly fast and can produce a dozen monstrous leaves before the end of summer. Longwood Gardens in Pennsylvania has produced a particularly beautiful hybrid with red upturned leaf edges.

Plants need full sun and still water. They are magnificent combined with tropical waterlilies and lotuses against a background of large waterside foliage plants like Chilean rhubarb.

Grow giant Amazon waterlily in submerged tubs with a capacity of at least 25 gallons (95L), and cover with 12 inches (30cm) of water. Propagation is by division in spring.

Zantedeschia aethiopica
(white calla lily)

Calla lilies are most often seen in white, but yellow, pink, purple, and red forms are also available.

Also known as arum lily, the white calla lily is one of the best marginal plants for both formal and informal water gardens, growing to 4 feet (1.2m) high. Its erect, spear-shaped green leaves and white hooded spadix lend an architectural quality to geometrically shaped pools and a hint of the tropics to informal pools. Though it grows all the way into Canada on the West Coast, in the Northeast it is not reliably hardy north of Washington, D.C. Yet in all locations it grows easily in containers, flowers in spring, and can be moved indoors at the approach of freezing weather. Other species of calla lily offer shades of yellow, pink, and red. These species have been bred to create beautiful hybrids, one of the best of which is named 'Kiwi' because of its New Zealand origins.

A special variety of calla, 'Green Goddess', can grow to 6 feet (1.8m) high. Its large, wavy, white flowers are tipped in green and measure up to 7 inches (17.5cm) long. It blooms later than the common white, usually in early summer. Plants prefer full sun but tolerate shade. They like a humus-rich soil and their roots in shallow water. Calla lilies are greatly valued by flower arrangers. Propagation is by division.

About
the
Author

Derek Fell is a writer and photographer who specializes in gardening, with an emphasis on step-by-step gardening concepts and garden design. He lives in Bucks County, Pennsylvania, at historic Cedaridge Farm, Tinicum Township, where he cultivates extensive award-winning flower and vegetable gardens that have been featured in *Architectural Digest, Garden Design, Beautiful Gardens, Gardens Illustrated, American Nurseryman,* and *Mid-Atlantic Country* magazines. Born and educated in England, he first worked for seven years with Europe's largest seed company, then moved to Pennsylvania in 1964 to work for Burpee Seeds as their catalog manager, a position he held for six years before taking on duties as executive director of the All-America Selections (the national seed trials) and the National Garden Bureau (an information office sponsored by the American seed industry). Now the author of more than fifty garden books and calendars, he has traveled widely throughout North America, also documenting gardens in Europe, Africa, New Zealand, and Asia. His most recent books are *Herb Gardening with Derek Fell, Bulb Gardening with Derek Fell,* and *Secrets of Monet's Garden*

A frequent contributor to *Architectural Digest* and *Woman's Day* magazines, Derek Fell is the winner of more awards from the Garden Writers Association of America than any other garden writer. He also worked as a consultant on gardening to the White House during the Ford Administration.

Wall calendars, greeting cards, and art posters featuring Derek Fell's photography are published worldwide. He has lectured on photography and the gardens of the great Impressionist painters at numerous art museums, including the Smithsonian Institution in Washington, D.C.; the Philadelphia Museum of Art and the Barnes Foundation, Philadelphia; and the Denver Art Museum, Colorado. He is also host of a regular garden show for the QVC cable television shopping channel, entitled *Step-by-Step Gardening,* which is plugged into fifty million homes.

Fell's highly acclaimed *Step-by-Step Gardening* mail-order perennial plant catalogs for Spring Hill Nurseries (North America's largest mail-order nursery) reach an audience of home gardeners estimated to be more than three million in spring and autumn. He is a former president of the Hobby Greenhouse Association, a former director of the Garden Writers Association of America, the president of the International Test Gardeners Association, and a cofounder of the American Gardening Association.

A complete list of published works follows.

Books by Derek Fell

(An asterisk indicates coauthorship.)

The White House Vegetable Garden. 1976, Exposition.

House Plants for Fun & Profit. 1978, Bookworm.

How to Photograph Flowers, Plants, & Landscapes. 1980, HP Books.

Vegetables: How to Select, Grow, and Enjoy. 1982, HP Books.

Annuals: How to Select, Grow, and Enjoy. 1983, HP Books.

Deerfield: An American Garden Through Four Seasons. 1986, Pidcock Press.

Trees & Shrubs. 1986, HP Books.

Garden Accents. 1987, Henry Holt. (*Inspired Garden* in the United Kingdom)

Discover Anguilla. 1988, Caribbean Concepts.

Home Landscaping. 1988, Simon & Schuster.

The One-Minute Gardener. 1988, Running Press.

A Kid's First Gardening Book. 1989, Running Press.

Three Year Garden Journal. 1989, Starwood.

Ornamental Grass Gardening. 1989, HP Books.

The Complete Garden Planning Manual. 1989, HP Books.

The Essential Gardener. 1990, Crown.

Essential Roses. 1990, Crown.

Essential Annuals. 1990, Crown.

Essential Bulbs. 1990, Crown.

Essential Perennials. 1990, Crown.

Essential Shrubs. 1990, Crown.

The Easiest Flower to Grow. 1990, Ortho.

550 Home Landscaping Ideas. 1991, Simon & Schuster.

Renoir's Garden. 1991, Simon & Schuster.

Beautiful Bucks County. 1991, Cedaridge.

The Encyclopedia of Ornamental Grasses. 1992, Smithmark.

The Encyclopedia of Flowers. 1993, Smithmark.

550 Perennial Garden Ideas. 1993, Simon & Schuster.

The Impressionist Garden. 1994, Crown.

Practical Gardening. 1995, Friedman/Fairfax.

Gardens of Philadelphia & the Delaware Valley. 1995, Temple University Press.

The Pennsylvania Gardener. 1995, Camino Books.

In the Garden with Derek. 1995, Camino Books.

Glorious Flowers. 1996, Friedman/Fairfax.

Perennial Gardening with Derek Fell. 1996, Friedman/Fairfax.

Vegetable Gardening with Derek Fell. 1996, Friedman/Fairfax

Derek Fell's Handy Garden Guides: Annuals. 1996, Friedman/Fairfax.

Derek Fell's Handy Garden Guides: Perennials. 1996, Friedman/Fairfax.

Derek Fell's Handy Garden Guides: Roses. 1996, Friedman/Fairfax.

Derek Fell's Handy Garden Guides: Bulbs. 1996, Friedman/Fairfax.

Herb Gardening with Derek Fell. 1997, Friedman/Fairfax.

Bulb Gardening with Derek Fell. 1997, Friedman/Fairfax.

Secrets of Monet's Garden. 1997, Friedman/Fairfax.

Calendars

Great Gardens (Portal)

Monet's Garden (Portal)

The Impressionist Garden (Portal)

The Gardening Year (Portal)

Perennials (Starwood)

Flowering Shrubs (Starwood)

Flowering Bulbs (Starwood)

Northeast Gardens Calendar (Starwood)

Mid-Atlantic Gardens Calendar (Starwood)

Southern Gardens Calendar (Starwood)

California Gardens Calendar (Starwood)

Pacific Northwest Gardens Calendar (Starwood)

Art Posters

Deerfield Garden (Portal)

Spring Garden (Portal)

Monet's Bridge (Portal)

Sources

The following companies sell aquatic plants and supplies by mail. An asterisk indicates that the company welcomes customers from Canada. You should also consider applying for membership in the Water Lily Society, Box 104, Buckeystown, MD 21717.

Lilypons Water Gardens
6800 Lilypons Road
Buckeystown, MD 21717-0010

Lilypons branch offices
also at:
P.O. Box 188
Brookshire, TX 77423

Box 1130
Thermal, CA 92274

*Maryland Aquatic
Nurseries Inc.
3427 North Furnace Road
Jerretsville, MD 21084

*Matterhorn Nursery Inc.
227 Summit Park Road
Spring Valley, NY 10977

North American Pond
Source Inc.
1301 Mermaid Lane
Wyndmoor, PA 19038

Santa Barbara Water
Gardens
160 East Mountain Drive
Santa Barbara, CA 93140

Slocum Water Gardens
1101 Cypress Gardens
Boulevard
Winter Haven, FL 33884-1932

Van Ness Water Gardens
2460 North Euclid
Avenue
Upland, CA 91784-1199

Waterford Gardens
74 East Allendale Road
Saddle River, NJ 07458

Water Lily World
2331 Goodloe Street
Houston, TX 77093

Water Ways Nursery
Route 2, Box 247
Lovettesville, VA 22080

*Wicklein's Water Gardens
1820 Cromwell Bridge
Road
Baltimore, MD 21234

*William Tricker
7125 Tanglewood Drive
Independence, OH 44131

PLANT HARDINESS ZONES

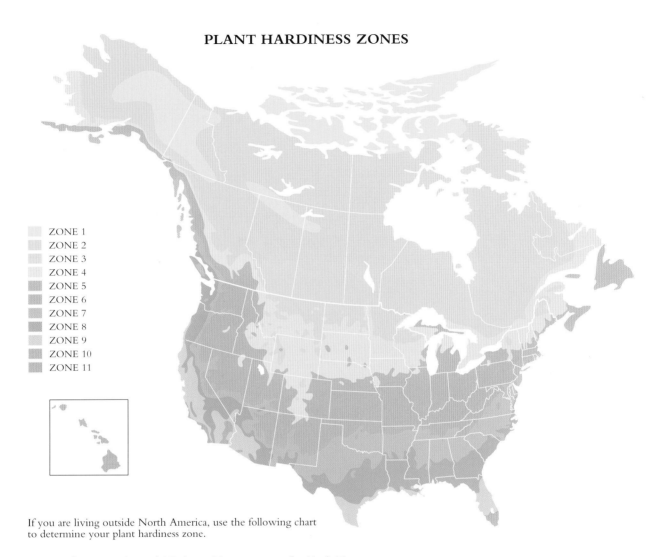

ZONE 1
ZONE 2
ZONE 3
ZONE 4
ZONE 5
ZONE 6
ZONE 7
ZONE 8
ZONE 9
ZONE 10
ZONE 11

If you are living outside North America, use the following chart
to determine your plant hardiness zone.

Range of Average Annual MinimumTemperatures for Each Zone

	Farenheit (°F)	Celsius (°C)
ZONE 1	Below -50°	Below -45.6°
ZONE 2	-50° to -40°	-45.6° to -40°
ZONE 3	-40° to -30°	-40° to -34.4°
ZONE 4	-30° to -20°	-34.4° to -28.9°
ZONE 5	-20° to -10°	-28.9° to -23.3°
ZONE 6	-10° to 0°	-23.3° to -17.8°
ZONE 7	0° to 10°	-17.8° to -12.2°
ZONE 8	10° to 20°	-12.2° to -6.7°
ZONE 9	20° to 30°	-6.7° to -1.1°
ZONE 10	30° to 40°	-1.1° to 4.4°
ZONE 11	Above 40°	Above 4.4°

Index